DOGS ON JUMPERS

First published in the United Kingdom in 2018 by
Pavilion
43 Great Ormond Street
London
WC1N 3HZ

ISBN 978-1-911216-95-7

A CIP catalogue record for this book is available from the
British Library.

10 9 8 7 6 5 4 3 2 1

Reproduction by Colourdepth
Printed and bound by Toppan Leefung Printing Ltd, China

This book can be ordered direct from the publisher at
www.pavilionbooks.com

DOGS ON JUMPERS

SALLY MUIR & JOANNA OSBORNE

PAVILION

DOGS ON JUMPERS 6
HOW TO USE THIS BOOK 8
KNIT YOUR OWN DOG 10

ADULT JUMPERS 14
Woman's raglan jumper 16
Woman's long and loose jumper 18
Man's jumper 20

Labrador 28
Lurcher 30
Beagle 32
Dalmatian 34
Pug 36
French Bulldog 38
Golden Retriever 40
Chihuahua 42
Springer Spaniel 44
Staffordshire Bull Terrier 46
Labradoodle 48
Jack Russell 50
Miniature Schnauzer 52
Whippet 54
Border Terrier 56
Border Collie 58
West Highland Terrier 60
Dachshund 62
Cave Canem
(Beware of the Dog) 64

CHILD AND BABY JUMPERS AND CARDIGANS 66
Child's jumper 68
Baby's raglan jumper 70
Baby's cardigan 72

West Highland Terrier 80
Dalmatian 82
Labrador 84
Dachshund 86
Pug 88
Border Collie 90
Jack Russell 92
Whippet 94

ACCESSORIES 96
Pug hat 100
Dalmatian onesie 102
Dachshund boots 106
Pug boots 108
Jack Russell scarf 110
Jack Russell boots 111
Dog coat 112
Patchwork baby blanket 114

GRAPHS 120
INDEX OF DOGS 140
ABBREVIATIONS 141
RESOURCES 143
ACKNOWLEDGEMENTS 143
MUIR & OSBORNE 144

DOGS ON JUMPERS

Dogs on Jumpers combines our two great interests: dogs and knitwear. We have been knitwear designers, as Muir and Osborne, for many years, and animals have appeared in our designs right from the beginning of our business. In the early days there was the Princess Diana sheep jumper and the Wolf in Sheep's Clothing design for *Cosmopolitan* magazine. Our first knitting book was *Pet Heaven: The Animal Accessory Bible*.

We appeared on *The Martha Stewart Show*, compèring a dog fashion show and demonstrating how to upcycle a cardigan into a dog coat. Then we decided to go three-dimensional with our first *Best in Show* book, *Knit Your Own Dog*. This was a remarkable success that encouraged us to write a further six books in the series. As with our *Best in Show* books, we are hoping that you use this book as inspiration and adapt our designs to your own particular dog.

We have designed for men, women, children, babies and even dogs, so if you are a keen knitter, your whole family can now wear Dogs on Jumpers.

HOW TO USE THIS BOOK

MAKING THE JUMPERS

There are three adult options and three child/baby options, each with its own master pattern, so the first decision to make is to choose the shape of the jumper:

- Woman's Raglan Jumper (page 16): this is neat and boxy.
- Woman's Long and Loose Jumper (page 18): this is exactly what it is, easy to wear and suits most body shapes.
- Man's Jumper (page 20): relaxed style, set-in sleeves.
- Child's Jumper (page 68): dropped shoulders, loose shape.
- Baby's Raglan Jumper (page 70): for up to age 3 years, raglan shape, similar to a sweatshirt.
- Baby's Cardigan (page 72): for up to age 6 months, set-in sleeves, easy cardigan.

The second decision is to choose the dog you would like to knit. There is a choice of 18 dogs – plus a slogan design – for the adult jumpers (see pages 22–27), and 8 dogs for the child and baby jumpers (see pages 76–79). Start by following the master pattern for your selected jumper. When working the front of the jumper, refer to the separate instructions and graph for your chosen dog breed (see index of dog breeds on page 140).

YARNS

The adult jumpers are worked in aran-weight yarn. We have used either Cascade 220 Aran or Debbie Bliss Luxury Tweed Aran yarn for the main jumper. The yarn quantities for the main colour are listed in the master patterns. For the dogs we have used mainly Cascade 220 Aran because of the superb colour range. The yarn requirements for each dog are listed with the dog breed.

Cascade yarn is readily available in the US; in the UK, you can buy it from www.woolwarehouse.co.uk, although any aran-weight yarn would be perfect.

For the child and baby knitwear, we recommend Erika Knight's British Blue Wool or British Blue 100. This lovely soft, airy yarn is available at most wool shops as well as online, but any double-knit weight would do.

DESIGN CHOICES

Our patterns are designed to be used as a template, to which you can then add details. There are two options for the rib: work in one colour throughout, or add a contrast edge to the back, front and sleeves. Both possibilities are included in the master patterns. The dog graph pattern can be started anywhere on the jumper. We have generally placed the dog in the middle of the front, slightly higher than the centre.

All of the dogs can be knitted directly onto the main colour of the jumper, or they can be framed inside a square or oval in a contrasting colour. The only exception is the Dachshund, which can be knitted onto a contrasting stripe running the full width of the jumper to accommodate its length.

A contrast square is much easier to work than an oval. We suggest knitting about 4 rows of contrast colour above and below the dog, and 3 contrast stitches on either side of the dog. For the oval, use graph paper to draw an oval around the dog, leaving about 3 stitches/4 rows between the dog's nose/tail and the edge of the oval.

LETTERING

We have included an alphabet for dog names and dog slogans (page 130). Follow the pattern for the Golden Retriever front for the positioning of a dog's name (page 40); the height of the lettering will remain the same, but the width of the name will vary. Using the alphabet provided, copy your dog's name onto graph paper and adjust the position as follows for a slogan jumper.

For slogan jumpers, copy the chosen letters onto graph paper, then count the stitches and rows. To position the slogan, refer to the index of dogs (page 140) and select the dog that is closest in size to your slogan. To centre the slogan, count the number of stitches, subtract these from the width of the jumper and divide by two. Use a small ball of contrast colour for each letter, and take the main colour across the back of the letter. If there are more than 3 stitches in the contrast colour, weave the main colour across the back of the letter using the Fair Isle method (see below).

INTARSIA METHOD

We recommend using the intarsia method for knitting the dogs, although you can take the main colour across the back of skinny legs, such as those of the Whippet. Use a small ball of yarn for each area of colour, otherwise the yarns will easily become tangled. When changing to a new colour, twist the yarns on the wrong side of the work to prevent holes from forming. When starting a new row, turn the knitting so that the yarns are hanging from it, untwisting them as much as possible. If you have several colours, you may occasionally have to reorganise the yarns at the back of the knitting.

FAIR ISLE METHOD

Use this method for skinny legs, Dalmatian spots and lettering. Begin knitting with the first colour, then drop this when you introduce the second colour. When you come to the first colour again, take it under the second colour to twist the yarns. When you come to the second colour again, take it over the first colour. If working over more than 3 stitches of the second colour, catch the first colour at the back of the work with the second colour so that the first colour strand is not floating loose. The secret is not to pull the strands on the wrong side of the work too tightly or the work will pucker.

EMBROIDERY STITCHES

Some of the dogs have a single stitch in a contrast colour for the eyes or nose. Rather than knitting this as part of the pattern, you can use the contrast colour to Swiss darn over the knitted stitch below.

French knots are used to make the eyes of many of the dogs. You can make the knots smaller or larger, as you wish.

SWISS DARNING

Thread a tapestry needle with yarn and insert it through the knitting from back to front, bringing it out at the bottom of the 'V' of the required stitch. Insert the needle from right to left under the two strands of yarn at the base of the stitch above, then take it back through the entry point. This makes a duplicate stitch over the original stitch. YouTube is a helpful source for tutorials if you need extra assistance.

FRENCH KNOTS

Thread a tapestry needle with yarn and insert it through the knitting from back to front. Wrap the yarn around the needle about three times, depending on the thickness of the yarn and how big you want the finished knot to be. To finish the knot, insert the needle back into the knitting no more than one stitch away from where you came out. Slowly pull the needle and ease the yarn through the wrapped loops to complete a French knot.

CHECKLIST
- Shape of jumper
- Dog breed
- Contrast edges or not
- Square, oval, stripe or dog only
- Lettering

KNIT YOUR OWN DOG

Feel free to play around with colours and markings, with the position of the dog on the jumper and with the shape of the background – square, oval or stripe. Among the graphs at the back of the book we have included an alphabet, so you can make up your own dog-related phrases, or add your dog's name or initials. These can also be added to the baby blanket if you want to personalise it. Here are our tips for knitting your own dog jumper.

COLOUR

We have chosen the colours we like, and that feel suitable for the breed, mainly using Cascade Yarns with their wide colour range. You can, of course, use any colour; make sure the colours are not too close to each other otherwise your dog may 'vanish'. Contrast between dog and background is important.

POSITION OF THE DOG ON THE JUMPER

We have designed the jumpers mainly with the dogs in the centre. This is a personal choice; you can move the dog up or down, or wrap the dog around the side of the jumper, knitting the head on the front and the tail end on the back of the jumper. The child's Dachshund pattern is a good example of an alternative position for the dog (see page 86).

KNITTING GRAPH PAPER

To create your own designs you will need knitting graph paper. There are plenty of sites online for sourcing knitting graph paper – we use the site www.theknittingsite.com. The 'squares' are oblong and reflect the shape of stitches.

CUSTOMISING THE GRAPHS

All dogs have their own markings. You can alter the markings to match your dog using knitting graph paper. If your dog has a longer body, for example, add a couple of stitches; for shorter legs, take off a couple of rows. The Labradoodle could be a Cockerpoo, for instance, by shortening the legs by a couple of rows and taking a couple of stitches out of the length of the body.

POSITION OF LETTERING ON THE JUMPER

When making a lettering jumper, use graph paper and copy the letters from the alphabet, leaving one or two stitches between each letter. For dog names, a space of 2–3cm (¾–1¼in) between the top of the letters and the start of the dog will make the name stand out but still feel part of the image.

BACKGROUND SHAPES

Some of the dogs are knitted on a square or oval in a contrasting colour. For the square, work 4 rows of colour before you start the dog and 4 rows after finishing the dog. Add about 3 stitches to either side of the dog in the contrast square colour. For the oval, using the Pug graph as an example (see page 126), copy the dog onto graph paper and draw an oval around the dog, leaving a few rows/stitches between the dog and the edge of the oval. Again, colour choice is important: make sure you have a strong contrast between the colours otherwise your dog may not stand out.

ADULT JUMPERS

We have three basic patterns: two for women and one for men. The Woman's Raglan Jumper is neat and boxy. The Woman's Long and Loose Jumper is exactly as described: easy to wear and suitable for most body shapes. The Man's Jumper is a relaxed style with set-in sleeves. All the adult jumpers are in aran-weight yarn in simple stocking stitch, so they are relatively quick to knit. The dogs are all knitted in intarsia, so it helps to have some experience of colour knitting. Once you have decided on the shape, choose your breed; all of the breeds are pictured on pages 22–27 to help you make your selection. Some breeds are more complicated than others. One-colour dogs – the Labrador, Lurcher, West Highland Terrier and Labradoodle – are the easiest to knit, but none of the dogs is particularly difficult.

WOMAN'S RAGLAN JUMPER

MEASUREMENTS

Small
Bust flat: 49cm (19¼in)
Length: 56cm (22in)

Medium
Bust flat: 51cm (20in)
Length: 59cm (23¼in)

Large
Bust flat: 53cm (21in)
Length: 59cm (23¼in)

MATERIALS
- Pair of 4mm (US 6) and 5mm (US 8) knitting needles if using Cascade yarn
- Pair of 3.75mm (US 5) and 4.5mm (US 7) knitting needles if using Debbie Bliss yarn
- Main colour (mc): Cascade 220 Aran or Debbie Bliss Luxury Tweed Aran yarn

Size	Small	Medium	Large
Cascade	475g (16½oz)	500g (17½oz)	525g (18½oz)
Debbie Bliss	450g (16oz)	475g (16½oz)	500g (17½oz)

- 10g (¼oz) of Cascade or Debbie Bliss yarn in contrast colour (optional)

TENSION
18 sts and 24 rows to 10cm (4in) measured over st st using 5mm (US 8) needles for Cascade yarn or 4.5mm (US 7) needles for Debbie Bliss yarn

DOG ON FRONT
All of the dogs are different shapes and colours. For yarn requirements and knitting instructions, refer to the index of dogs on page 140. This will direct you to the instructions and graph for your chosen breed.

BACK
With smaller needles and mc, cast on 90 [94, 98] sts.
Work 10 rows k2, p2 rib.
NOTE: For version with contrast edge, use contrast yarn to cast on and work first rib row, then change to mc to complete rib.
Change to larger needles.
Beg with a k row, continue in st st until back measures 34 [36, 36] cm (13½ [14¼, 14¼] in), ending on a p row.
SHAPE ARMHOLES:
Cast off 3 [4, 4] sts at beg of next 2 rows. (84 [86, 90] sts)
Dec 1 st at each end of next and every other row 26 [27, 27] times, ending on a p row. (32 [32, 36] sts)

Leave rem 32 [32, 36] sts on a holder for neck edge.

FRONT
Work as for back to armhole shaping, positioning and knitting the dog as instructed for your chosen dog breed (see index of dogs, page 140).
Continue in st st until front measures 34 [36, 36] cm (13½ [14¼, 14¼] in), ending on a p row.
SHAPE ARMHOLES:
Cast off 3 [4, 4] sts at beg of next 2 rows. (84 [86, 90] sts)
Dec 1 st at each end of next and every other row 18 [18, 19] times, ending on a p row. (48 [50, 52] sts)

SHAPE FRONT NECK:
With RS facing, k2tog, k15 [16, 17], turn, leaving rem sts on a holder.
Work each side separately:
Dec 1 st at beg of next row and at neck edge of every following row 5 [5, 7] times, and then at neck edge of every other row 3 times, and **at the same time** continue raglan shaping by dec 1 st at armhole edge of every other row.
With RS facing, slip centre 14 sts onto a holder for neck edge, rejoin yarn and k to last 2 sts, k2tog.
Complete to match first side, reversing shaping.

SLEEVES (MAKE 2)

With smaller needles, cast on
38 [42, 44] sts and work rib as for back.
Change to larger needles.
Beg with a k row, continue in st st,
shaping sides by inc 1 st at each
end of next and every following
6th row 15 times. (68 [72, 74] sts)
Continue straight until sleeve
measures 48 [48, 50] cm
(19 [19, 19¾] in), ending on a p row.
SHAPE SLEEVE TOP:
Cast off 3 [4, 4] sts at beg of next
2 rows. (62 [64, 66] sts)
Dec 1 st at each end of next and
every other row 26 [27, 27] times.
(10 [10, 12] sts)
Leave rem 10 [10, 12] sts on a holder
for neck edge.

MAKING UP

Block each piece and, using a
warm iron and cloth, press all parts
except ribbing. Sew in ends. Using
backstitch or mattress stitch, sew
up raglan seams but leave left back
raglan open.

NECK EDGE

With smaller needles and mc and RS
facing, pick up 10 [10, 12] sts across
top of left sleeve, 15 [15, 16] sts down
left front neck shaping, 14 sts across
centre front, 15 [15, 16] sts up right
front neck shaping, 10 [10, 12] sts
across top of right sleeve and
32 [32, 36] sts across back neck.
(96 [96, 106] sts)

Work 6 rows k2, p2 rib.
Cast off loosely in rib.

TO FINISH

Using backstitch or mattress stitch,
sew up remaining raglan seam and
neck edge. Sew up side and sleeve
seams. Press with a damp cloth.

WOMAN'S LONG AND LOOSE JUMPER

MEASUREMENTS

Small
Bust flat: 58cm (23in)
Length: 66cm (26in)

Medium
Bust flat: 62cm (24½in)
Length: 68cm (26¾in)

Large
Bust flat: 66cm (26in)
Length: 70cm (27½in)

MATERIALS

- Pair of 4mm (US 6) and 5mm (US 8) knitting needles if using Cascade yarn
- Pair of 3.75mm (US 5) and 4.5mm (US 7) knitting needles if using Debbie Bliss yarn
- Main colour (mc): Cascade 220 Aran or Debbie Bliss Luxury Tweed Aran yarn

Size	Small	Medium	Large
Cascade	575g (20oz)	600g (21oz)	625g (22oz)
Debbie Bliss	525g (18½oz)	550g (19¼oz)	575g (20oz)

- 10g (¼oz) of Cascade or Debbie Bliss yarn in contrast colour (optional)

TENSION
18 sts and 24 rows to 10cm (4in) measured over st st using 5mm (US 8) needles for Cascade yarn or 4.5mm (US 7) needles for Debbie Bliss yarn

DOG ON FRONT
All of the dogs are different shapes and colours. For yarn requirements and knitting instructions, refer to the index of dogs on page 140. This will direct you to the instructions and graph for your chosen breed.

BACK
With smaller needles and mc, cast on 106 [114, 122] sts.
Work 20 rows k2, p2 rib.
NOTE: For version with contrast edge, use contrast yarn to cast on and work first rib row, then change to mc to complete rib.
Change to larger needles.
Beg with a k row, continue in st st until back measures 43 [45, 47] cm (17 [17¾, 18½] in), ending on a p row.
SHAPE ARMHOLES:
Cast off 8 sts at beg of next 2 rows.
(90 [98, 106] sts)

Continue straight until armhole measures 20cm (8in), ending on a p row.
SHAPE SHOULDERS:
Next row (RS): Cast off 6 [7, 8] sts, k24 [27, 30] including st used to cast off, turn, leaving rem sts on a holder. Work each side separately:
Next row (WS): Dec 1 st at neck edge, p to end.
Next row (RS): Cast off 7 [8, 9] sts, k to end.
Next row (WS): Dec 1 st at neck edge, p to end.
Next row (RS): Cast off 7 [8, 9] sts, k to end.

Next row (WS): Dec 1 st at neck edge, p to end.
Next row (RS): Cast off rem 7 [8, 9] sts. With RS facing, slip centre 30 sts onto a holder for neck edge, rejoin yarn and k to end. Complete to match first side, reversing shaping.

FRONT
Work as for back to armhole shaping, positioning and knitting the dog as instructed for your chosen dog breed (see index of dogs, page 140).
SHAPE ARMHOLES:
Cast off 8 sts at beg of next 2 rows.
(90 [98, 106] sts)

Continue straight until armhole measures 18 rows less than back to shoulder, ending on a p row.

SHAPE FRONT NECK:
With RS facing, k38 [42, 46], turn, leaving rem sts on a holder.
Work each side separately:
Dec 1 st at neck edge of every row 6 times, and then at neck edge of every other row 5 times. (27 [31, 35] sts)
Work 1 row straight, so front matches back at shoulder, ending on a p row.

SHAPE SHOULDER:
Next row (RS): Cast off 6 [7, 8] sts, k to end.
Next row (WS): Purl.
Next row (RS): Cast off 7 [8, 9] sts, k to end.
Next row (WS): Purl.
Next row (RS): Cast off 7 [8, 9] sts, k to end.
Next row (WS): Purl.
Next row (RS): Cast off rem 7 [8, 9] sts.

With RS facing, slip centre 14 sts onto a holder, rejoin yarn and k to end.
Work 1 row, then complete to match first side, reversing shaping.

SLEEVES (MAKE 2)
With smaller needles, cast on 40 sts and work rib as for back.
Change to larger needles.
Beg with a k row, continue in st st, shaping sides by inc 1 st at each end of next and every following 4th row 10 times, and then every 6th row 8 times. (76 sts)
Continue straight until sleeve measures 46 [47, 47] cm (18 [18½, 18½] in).
Cast off rem sts.

MAKING UP
Block each piece and, using a warm iron and cloth, press all parts except ribbing. Sew in ends. Using backstitch or mattress stitch, sew right shoulder together.

NECK EDGE
With smaller needles and mc and RS facing, starting at left front shoulder pick up 24 sts down left front neck shaping, 14 sts across centre front, 24 sts up right front neck shaping, 6 sts down right back shaping, 34 sts across back neck and 6 sts up left back shaping. (104 sts)
Work 6 rows k2, p2 rib.
Cast off loosely in rib.

TO FINISH
Using backstitch or mattress stitch, sew left shoulder together and neck edge. Sew cast-off edge of sleeve around armhole, and sew up side and sleeve seams. Press with a damp cloth.

MAN'S JUMPER

MEASUREMENTS

Small
Chest flat: 56cm (22in)
Length: 70cm (27½in)

Medium
Chest flat: 60cm (23½in)
Length: 72cm (28¼in)

Large
Chest flat: 63cm (24¾in)
Length: 72cm (28¼in)

MATERIALS

- Pair of 4mm (US 6) and 5mm (US 8) knitting needles if using Cascade yarn
- Pair of 3.75mm (US 5) and 4.5mm (US 7) knitting needles if using Debbie Bliss yarn
- Main colour (mc): Cascade 220 Aran or Debbie Bliss Luxury Tweed Aran yarn

Size	Small	Medium	Large
Cascade	575g (20oz)	600g (21oz)	625g (22oz)
Debbie Bliss	525g (18½oz)	550g (19¼oz)	575g (20oz)

- 10g (¼oz) of Cascade or Debbie Bliss yarn in contrast colour (optional)

TENSION
18 sts and 24 rows to 10cm (4in) measured over st st using 5mm (US 8) needles for Cascade yarn or 4.5mm (US 7) needles for Debbie Bliss yarn

DOG ON FRONT
All of the dogs are different shapes and colours. For yarn requirements and knitting instructions, refer to the index of dogs on page 140. This will direct you to the instructions and graph for your chosen breed.

BACK
With smaller needles and mc, cast on 104 [110, 116] sts.
Work 16 rows k2, p2 rib.
NOTE: For version with contrast edge, use contrast yarn to cast on and work first rib row, then change to mc to complete rib.
Change to larger needles.
Beg with a k row, continue in st st until back measures 43 [45, 45] cm (17 [17¾, 17¾] in), ending on a p row.
SHAPE ARMHOLES:
Cast off 5 sts at beg of next 2 rows. *(94 [100, 106] sts)*
Dec 1 st at each end of next 5 rows, and then at each end of every other row 6 [7, 8] times. *(72 [76, 80] sts)*
Continue straight until armhole measures 24cm (9½in), ending on a p row.
SHAPE SHOULDERS:
Next row (RS): Cast off 5 [5, 6] sts, k17 [19, 20] including st used to cast off, turn, leaving rem sts on a holder.
Work each side separately:
Next row (WS): Dec 1 st at neck edge, p to end.
Next row (RS): Cast off 5 [5, 6] sts, k to end.
Next row (WS): Dec 1 st at neck edge, p to end.
Next row (RS): Cast off 5 [6, 6] sts, k to end.
Next row (WS): Purl.
Next row (RS): Cast off rem 5 [6, 6] sts.
With RS facing, slip centre 28 sts onto a holder for neck edge, rejoin yarn and k to end. Complete to match first side, reversing shaping.

FRONT
Work as for back to armhole shaping, positioning and knitting the dog as instructed for your chosen dog breed (see index of dogs, page 140).
SHAPE ARMHOLES:
Work as for back, but continue in st st until armhole measures 17cm (6¾in), ending on a p row.
SHAPE FRONT NECK:
With RS facing, k29 [31, 33], turn, leaving rem sts on a holder.
Work each side separately:
Dec 1 st at neck edge of every row 6 times, and then at neck edge of every

other row 3 times. *(20 [22, 24] sts)*
Continue straight until front matches back at shoulder, ending on a p row.

SHAPE SHOULDER:

Next row (RS): Cast off 5 [5, 6] sts, k to end.

Next row (WS): Purl.

Next row (RS): Cast off 5 [5, 6] sts, k to end.

Next row (WS): Purl.

Next row (RS): Cast off 5 [6, 6] sts, k to end.

Next row (WS): Purl.

Next row (RS): Cast off rem 5 [6, 6] sts.

With RS facing, slip centre 14 sts onto a holder, rejoin yarn and k to end. Complete to match first side, reversing shaping.

SLEEVES (MAKE 2)

With smaller needles, cast on 44 sts and work rib as for back.

Change to larger needles.
Beg with a k row, continue in st st, shaping sides by inc 1 st at each end of next and every following 8th [7th, 7th] row 13 [14, 16] times. *(70 [72, 76] sts)*
Continue straight until sleeve measures 52 [52, 54] cm (20½ [20½, 21¼] in), ending on a p row.

SHAPE SLEEVE TOP:

Cast off 5 sts at beg of next 2 rows. *(60 [62, 66] sts)*
Dec 1 st at each end of next 5 [5, 6] rows. *(50 [52, 54] sts)*
Dec 1 st at each end of every other row 13 times. *(24 [26, 28] sts)*
Dec 1 st at each end of every row 4 times. *(16 [18, 20] sts)*
Cast off rem sts.

MAKING UP

Block each piece and, using a warm iron and cloth, press all parts

except ribbing. Sew in ends. Using backstitch or mattress stitch, sew right shoulder together.

NECK EDGE

With smaller needles and mc and RS facing, starting at left front shoulder pick up 20 sts down left front neck shaping, 14 sts across centre front, 20 sts up right front neck shaping, 6 sts down right back shaping, 28 sts across back neck and 5 sts up left back shaping. *(92 sts)*
Work 8 rows k2, p2 rib.
Cast off loosely in rib.

TO FINISH

Using backstitch or mattress stitch, sew left shoulder together and neck edge. Set in sleeves and sew up side and sleeve seams. Press with a damp cloth.

Labrador

PAGE 28

Lurcher

PAGE 30

Beagle

PAGE 32

Dalmatian

PAGE 34

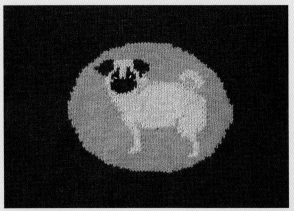

Pug

PAGE 36

French Bulldog

PAGE 38

Golden Retriever

PAGE 40

Chihuahua

PAGE 42

Springer Spaniel

PAGE 44

Staffordshire Bull Terrier

PAGE 46

Labradoodle

PAGE 48

Jack Russell

PAGE 50

Miniature
Schnauzer

PAGE 52

Whippet

PAGE 54

Border Terrier

PAGE 56

Border Collie

PAGE 58

West Highland Terrier

PAGE 60

Dachshund

PAGE 62

Cave Canem
(Beware of the Dog)

PAGE 64

LABRADOR

MATERIALS
- Main colour: Debbie Bliss Luxury Tweed Aran in 54 Sky (mc); see jumper pattern for quantity
- 15g (½oz) of Cascade 220 in 8555 Black (bl)
- Tiny amount of aran-weight yarn in brown (br) for eye

GRAPH
See page 125

WOMAN'S RAGLAN JUMPER (PAGE 16)
Continue in st st until front measures 19 [20, 20] cm (7½ [8, 8] in), ending on a p row.
Follow graph for Labrador.
Row 1: K24 [26, 28] mc, k3bl, k28mc, k3bl, k32 [34, 36] mc.
Continue graph pattern until dog is finished.

WOMAN'S LONG AND LOOSE JUMPER (PAGE 18)
Continue in st st until front measures 29 [30, 31] cm (11½ [11¾, 12¼] in), ending on a p row.
Follow graph for Labrador.
Row 1: K32 [36, 40] mc, k3bl, k28mc, k3bl, k40 [44, 48] mc.
Continue graph pattern until dog is finished.

MAN'S JUMPER (PAGE 20)
Continue in st st until front measures 29 [29, 30] cm (11½ [11½, 11¾] in), ending on a p row.
Follow graph for Labrador.
Row 1: K31 [34, 37] mc, k3bl, k28mc, k3bl, k39 [42, 45] mc.
Continue graph pattern until dog is finished.

FINISHING DETAILS
Eye: With br, make a 3-loop French knot for eye.

LURCHER

MATERIALS
- Main colour: Cascade 220 Heathers in 9450 Smoke Heather (mc); see jumper pattern for quantity
- Contrast colour: 50g (2oz) of Cascade 220 Heathers in 4002 Jet – charcoal (ch)
- 15g (½oz) of Rowan Kidsilk Haze in 00664 Steel and 00639 Anthracite (mohair – mo) – use FOUR strands together throughout (TWO strands of each colour)

GRAPH
See page 125

WOMAN'S RAGLAN JUMPER (PAGE 16)
This is an example for knitting the Lurcher without a square.
Continue in st st until front measures 21 [22, 22] cm (8¼ [8¾, 8¾] in), ending on a p row.
Follow graph for Lurcher.
Row 1: K46 [48, 50] mc, k2mo, k42 [44, 46] mc.
Continue graph pattern until dog is finished.

WOMAN'S LONG AND LOOSE JUMPER (PAGE 18)
This is an example for knitting the Lurcher without a square.
Continue in st st until front measures 32 [32, 33] cm (12½ [12½, 13] in), ending on a p row.
Follow graph for Lurcher.
Row 1: K54 [58, 62] mc, k2mo, k50 [54, 58] mc.
Continue graph pattern until dog is finished.

MAN'S JUMPER (PAGE 20)
Our Lurcher is knitted on a contrast square. Continue in st st until front measures 31 [32, 33] cm (12¼ [12½, 13] in), ending on a p row.
NOTE: For version without a contrast square, work all ch sts in mc.
Row 1: K30 [33, 36] mc, k44ch, k30 [33, 36] mc.
Work 5 rows st st, colours as set.
Then follow graph for Lurcher.
Row 7: K30 [33, 36] mc, k23ch, k2mo, k19ch, k30 [33, 36] mc.
Continue graph pattern until dog is finished.
Work 7 rows to match bottom of square, ending on a k row.
Continue in mc.

BEAGLE

MATERIALS
- Main colour: Cascade 220 in 8555 Black (mc); see jumper pattern for quantity
- Contrast colour: 50g (2oz) of Cascade 220 Heathers in 9451 Lake Chelan Heather – green (gn)
- 15g (½oz) of Cascade 220 in 8505 White (wh)
- 10g (¼oz) of Cascade 220 in 2415 Sunflower – gold (gd)
- 10g (¼oz) of Cascade 220 in 8555 Black (bl)

GRAPH
See page 120

WOMAN'S RAGLAN JUMPER (PAGE 16)
Our Beagle is knitted on a contrast square. Continue in st st until front measures 20 [21, 21] cm (8 [8¼, 8¼] in), ending on a k row.
NOTE: For version without a contrast square, work all gn sts in mc.
Row 1: P17 [19, 21] mc, p56gn, p17 [19, 21] mc.
Work 2 rows st st, colours as set. Then follow graph for Beagle.
Row 4: K17 [19, 21] mc, k35gn, k3wh, k18gn, k17 [19, 21] mc.
Continue graph pattern until dog is finished.
Work 3 rows to match bottom of square, ending on a k row.
Continue in mc.

WOMAN'S LONG AND LOOSE JUMPER (PAGE 18)
This is an example for knitting the Beagle without a square.
Continue in st st until front measures 32 [33, 34] cm (12½ [13, 13½] in), ending on a p row.
Follow graph for Beagle.
Row 1: K61 [65, 69] mc, k3wh, k42 [46, 50] mc.
Continue graph pattern until dog is finished.

MAN'S JUMPER (PAGE 20)
This is an example for knitting the Beagle without a square.
Continue in st st until front measures 32 [32, 33] cm (12½ [12½, 13] in), ending on a p row.
Follow graph for Beagle.
Row 1: K60 [63, 66] mc, k3wh, k41 [44, 47] mc.
Continue graph pattern until dog is finished.

DALMATIAN

MATERIALS

- Main colour: Cascade 220 Heathers in 8836 Stonewash – blue lovat (mc); see jumper pattern for quantity
- 15g (½oz) of Cascade 220 in 8505 White (wh)
- 10g (¼oz) of Cascade 220 in 8555 Black (bl)

GRAPH

See page 122

WOMAN'S RAGLAN JUMPER (PAGE 16)

Continue in st st until front measures 19 [20, 20] cm (7½ [8, 8] in), ending on a p row.

Follow graph for Dalmatian.

Row 1: K24 [26, 28] mc, k3wh, k28mc, k3wh, k32 [34, 36] mc.

Continue graph pattern until dog is finished.

WOMAN'S LONG AND LOOSE JUMPER (PAGE 18)

Continue in st st until front measures 29 [30, 31] cm (11½ [11¾, 12¼] in), ending on a p row.

Follow graph for Dalmatian.

Row 1: K32 [36, 40] mc, k3wh, k28mc, k3wh, k40 [44, 48] mc.

Continue graph pattern until dog is finished.

MAN'S JUMPER (PAGE 20)

Continue in st st until front measures 29 [29, 30] cm (11½ [11½, 11¾] in), ending on a p row.

Follow graph for Dalmatian.

Row 1: K31 [34, 37] mc, k3wh, k28mc, k3wh, k39 [42, 45] mc.

Continue graph pattern until dog is finished.

PUG

MATERIALS
- Main colour: Cascade 220 Heathers in 4002 Jet – charcoal (mc); see jumper pattern for quantity
- Contrast colour: 50g (2oz) of Cascade 220 Heathers in 9325 Westpoint Blue Heather – sky blue (bu)
- 20g (¾oz) of Cascade 220 Heathers in 2442 Fog Hatt – oatmeal (oa)
- 5g (⅛oz) of Cascade 220 Heathers in 4002 Jet – charcoal (ch)
- Tiny amount of Cascade 220 in 8555 Black (bl) for eyes
- Tiny amount of Cascade 220 in 8505 White (wh) for eyes

GRAPH
See page 126

WOMAN'S RAGLAN JUMPER (PAGE 16)
This is an example for knitting the Pug without an oval.
Continue in st st until front measures 23 [24, 24] cm (9 [9½, 9½] in), ending on a p row.
Follow graph pattern for Pug.
Row 1: K30 [32, 34] mc, k3oa, k16mc, k3oa, k38 [40, 42] mc.
Continue graph pattern until dog is finished.

WOMAN'S LONG AND LOOSE JUMPER (PAGE 18)
Our Pug is knitted on a contrast oval.
Continue in st st until front measures 27 [28, 29] cm (10¾ [11, 11½] in), ending on a k row.
NOTE: For version without a contrast oval, work all bu sts in mc.
Follow graph for Pug in oval.
Row 1: P46 [50, 54] mc, p14bu, p46 [50, 54] mc.
Continue to follow graph for oval.
START OF PUG:
Row 8: K35 [39, 43] mc, k3bu, k3oa, k16bu, k3oa, k11bu, k35 [39, 43] mc.
Continue graph pattern until dog is finished, then follow graph for last 7 rows of oval, ending on a k row.
Continue in mc.

MAN'S JUMPER (PAGE 20)
This is an example for knitting the Pug without an oval.
Continue in st st until front measures 30 [30, 31] cm (11¾ [11¾, 12¼] in), ending on a p row.
Follow graph for Pug.
Row 1: K37 [40, 43] mc, k3oa, k16mc, k3oa, k45 [48, 51] mc.
Continue graph pattern until dog is finished.

FINISHING DETAILS
Eyes: With bl, make a 3-loop French knot for each eye and sew a small slanting stitch on top in wh.

FRENCH BULLDOG

MATERIALS

- Main colour: Cascade 220 Heathers in 2442 Fog Hatt – oatmeal (mc); see jumper pattern for quantity
- 15g (½oz) of Cascade 220 Heathers in 4002 Jet – charcoal (ch)
- 5g (⅛oz) of Cascade 220 in 8505 White (wh)
- 5g (⅛oz) of Cascade 220 in 4192 Soft Pink (pk)
- Tiny amount of Cascade 220 in 8555 Black (bl) for eyes

GRAPH

See page 123

WOMAN'S RAGLAN JUMPER (PAGE 16)

Continue in st st until front measures 20 [21, 21] cm (8 [8¼, 8¼] in), ending on a p row.

Follow graph for French Bulldog.

Row 1: K36 [38, 40] mc, k3ch, k12mc, k3ch, k36 [38, 40] mc.

Continue graph pattern until dog is finished.

WOMAN'S LONG AND LOOSE JUMPER (PAGE 18)

Continue in st st until front measures 30 [31, 32] cm (11¾ [12¼, 12½] in), ending on a p row.

Follow graph for French Bulldog.

Row 1: K44 [48, 52] mc, k3ch, k12mc, k3ch, k44 [48, 52] mc.

Continue graph pattern until dog is finished.

MAN'S JUMPER (PAGE 20)

Continue in st st until front measures 31 [31, 32] cm (12¼ [12¼, 12½] in), ending on a p row.

Follow graph for French Bulldog.

Row 1: K43 [46, 49] mc, k3ch, k12mc, k3ch, k43 [46, 49] mc.

Continue graph pattern until dog is finished.

FINISHING DETAILS

Eyes: With bl, make a 3-loop French knot for each eye and sew a small slanting stitch on top in wh.

GOLDEN RETRIEVER

MATERIALS

- Main colour: Cascade 220 Heathers in 9325 in Westpoint Blue Heather – sky blue (mc); see jumper pattern for quantity
- 15g (½oz) of Cascade 220 in 9499 Sand – fawn (fn)
- Small amount of Cascade 220 Heathers in 4002 Jet – charcoal (ch) for lettering
- Tiny amount of Cascade 220 in 8555 Black (bl) for eye and nose
- Small amount of aran-weight yarn for collar (optional)
- Pair of 4mm (US 6) knitting needles for collar (optional)

GRAPHS

See page 123 for dog
See page 130 for lettering

WOMAN'S RAGLAN JUMPER (PAGE 16)

NOTE: There is no room for lettering on the raglan jumper.
Continue in st st until front measures 20 [21, 21] cm (8 [8¼, 8¼] in), ending on a p row.
Follow graph for Golden Retriever.
Row 1: K29 [31, 33] mc, k3fn, k27mc, k3fn, k28 [30, 32] mc.
Continue graph pattern until dog is finished.

WOMAN'S LONG AND LOOSE JUMPER (PAGE 18)

Continue in st st until front measures 20 [21, 22] cm (8 [8¼, 8¾] in), ending on a p row.
Follow graph for lettering; Hugo is an example.
Row 1: K34 [38, 42] mc, k3ch, k9mc, k4ch, k8mc, k3ch, k5mc, k2ch, k6mc k2ch, k30 [34, 38] mc.
Continue graph pattern until lettering is finished, ending on a p row.
Work 6 rows st st, ending on a p row.
Follow graph for Golden Retriever.
Next row: K37 [41, 45] mc, k3fn, k27mc, k3fn, k36 [40, 44] mc.
Continue graph pattern until dog is finished.

MAN'S JUMPER (PAGE 20)

Continue in st st until front measures 20 [20, 21] cm (8 [8, 8¼] in), ending on a p row.
Follow graph for lettering; Hugo is an example.
Row 1: K33 [36, 39] mc, k3ch, k9mc, k4ch, k8mc, k3ch, k5mc, k2ch, k6mc, k2ch, k29 [32, 35] mc.
Continue graph pattern until lettering is finished, ending on a p row.
Work 6 rows st st, ending on a p row.
Follow graph for Golden Retriever.
Next row: K36 [39, 42] mc, k3fn, k27mc, k3fn, k35 [38, 41] mc.
Continue graph pattern until dog is finished.

FINISHING DETAILS

Eye: With bl, make a 3-loop French knot for eye.
Collar: With 4mm (US 6) needles and collar colour, cast on 28 sts and knit 2 rows. Cast off. Push each end into the side of the dog's neck, and sew collar ends together on reverse side of jumper (optional, see page 23).

CHIHUAHUA

MATERIALS
- Main colour: Debbie Bliss Luxury Tweed Aran in 15 Charcoal (mc); see jumper pattern for quantity
- 15g (½oz) of Cascade 220 in 9499 Sand – fawn (fn)
- 5g (⅛oz) of Cascade 220 in 4192 Soft Pink (pk)
- Tiny amount of Cascade 220 in 8555 Black (bl) for eyes and nose

GRAPH
See page 121

WOMAN'S RAGLAN JUMPER (PAGE 16)
Continue in st st until front measures 21 [22, 22] cm (8¼ [8¾, 8¾] in), ending on a p row.
Follow graph for Chihuahua.
Row 1: K29 [31, 33] mc, k2fn, k18mc, k2fn, k39 [41, 43] mc.
Continue graph pattern until dog is finished.

WOMAN'S LONG AND LOOSE JUMPER (PAGE 18)
Continue in st st until front measures 32 [33, 34] cm (12½ [13, 13½] in), ending on a p row.
Follow graph for Chihuahua.
Row 1: K37 [41, 45] mc, k2fn, k18mc, k2fn, k47 [51, 55] mc.
Continue graph pattern until dog is finished.

MAN'S JUMPER (PAGE 20)
Continue in st st until front measures 32 [32, 33] cm (12½ [12½, 13] in), ending on a p row.
Follow graph for Chihuahua.
Row 1: K36 [39, 42] mc, k2fn, k18mc, k2fn, k46 [49, 52] mc.
Continue graph pattern until dog is finished.

FINISHING DETAILS
Eyes: With bl, make a 4-loop French knot for each eye.

SPRINGER SPANIEL

MATERIALS
- Main colour: Cascade 220 in 9635 Mineral Blue (mc); see jumper pattern for quantity
- 15g (½oz) of Cascade 220 in 2403 Chocolate – mahogany (ma)
- 10g (¼oz) of Cascade 220 in 8505 White (wh)
- Tiny amount of Cascade 220 in 8555 Black (bl) for eye and nose

GRAPH
See page 127

WOMAN'S RAGLAN JUMPER (PAGE 16)
Continue in st st until front measures 21 [22, 22] cm (8¼ [8¾, 8¾] in), ending on a p row.
Follow graph for Springer Spaniel.
Row 1: K29 [31, 33] mc, k3ma, k26mc, k3wh, k29 [31, 33] mc.
Continue graph pattern until dog is finished.

WOMAN'S LONG AND LOOSE JUMPER (PAGE 18)
Continue in st st until front measures 32 [33, 34] cm (12½ [13, 13½] in), ending on a p row.
Follow graph for Springer Spaniel.
Row 1: K37 [41, 45] mc, k3ma, k26mc, k3wh, k37 [41, 45] mc.
Continue graph pattern until dog is finished.

MAN'S JUMPER (PAGE 20)
Continue in st st until front measures 32 [32, 33] cm (12½ [12½, 13] in), ending on a p row.
Follow graph for Springer Spaniel.
Row 1: K36 [39, 42] mc, k3ma, k26mc, k3wh, k36 [39, 42] mc.
Continue graph pattern until dog is finished.

FINISHING DETAILS
Eye: With bl, make a 3-loop French knot for eye.

STAFFORDSHIRE BULL TERRIER

MATERIALS

- Main colour: Debbie Bliss Luxury Tweed Aran in 52 Lavender (mc); see jumper pattern for quantity
- Contrast colour: 10g (¼oz) of Cascade 220 Heathers in 2442 Fog Hatt – oatmeal (oa)
- 20g (¾oz) of Cascade 220 Heathers in 2442 Fog Hatt – oatmeal (oa)
- 15g (½oz) of Cascade 220 Heathers in 9465 Burnt Orange – brown (br)
- 5g (⅛oz) of Cascade 220 in 8505 White (wh)
- Tiny amount of Cascade 220 in 8555 Black (bl) for eye and nose

GRAPH

See page 127

WOMAN'S RAGLAN JUMPER (PAGE 16)

This is an example for knitting the Staffordshire Bull Terrier without a square.

Continue in st st until front measures 20 [21, 21] cm (8 [8¼, 8¼] in), ending on a p row.

Follow graph for Staffordshire Bull Terrier.

Row 1: K38 [40, 42] mc, k3br, k49 [51, 53] mc.

Continue graph pattern until dog is finished.

WOMAN'S LONG AND LOOSE JUMPER (PAGE 18)

This is an example for knitting the Staffordshire Bull Terrier without a square.

Continue in st st until front measures 30 [31, 32] cm (11¾ [12¼, 12½] in), ending on a p row.

Follow graph for Staffordshire Bull Terrier.

Row 1: K46 [50, 54] mc, k3br, k57 [61, 65] mc.

Continue graph pattern until dog is finished.

MAN'S JUMPER (PAGE 20)

Our Staffordshire Bull Terrier is knitted on a contrast square.

Continue in st st until front measures 29.5 [31, 31] cm (11¾ [12¼, 12¼] in), ending on a p row.

NOTE: For version without a contrast square, work all oa sts in mc.

Row 1: K23 [26, 29] mc, k58oa, k23 [26, 29] mc.

Work 3 rows st st, colours as set.

Follow graph for Staffordshire Bull Terrier.

Row 5: K23 [26, 29] mc, k22oa, k3br, k33oa, k23 [26, 29] mc.

Continue graph pattern until dog is finished.

Work 4 rows to match bottom of square, ending on a k row.

Continue in mc.

FINISHING DETAILS

Eye: With bl, make a 3-loop French knot for eye.

LABRADOODLE

MATERIALS
- Main colour: Cascade 220 in 8393 Navy (mc); see jumper pattern for quantity
- Contrast edge: 10g (¼oz) of Cascade 220 in 8010 Natural – cream (cr)
- 15g (½oz) of Drops Alpaca Bouclé in 0100 Off White (ow)
- Tiny amount of Cascade 220 in 8555 Black (bl) for eyes and nose

GRAPH
See page 124

WOMAN'S RAGLAN JUMPER (PAGE 16)
Continue in st st until front measures 20 [21, 21] cm (8 [8¼, 8¼] in), ending on a p row.
Follow graph for Labradoodle.
Row 1: K50 [52, 54] mc, k3ow, k37 [39, 41] mc.
Continue graph pattern until dog is finished.

WOMAN'S LONG AND LOOSE JUMPER (PAGE 18)
Continue in st st until front measures 30 [31, 32] cm (11¾ [12¼, 12½] in), ending on a p row.
Follow graph for Labradoodle.
Row 1: K58 [62, 66] mc, k3ow, k45 [49, 53] mc.
Continue graph pattern until dog is finished.

MAN'S JUMPER (PAGE 20)
Continue in st st until front measures 31 [31, 32] cm (12¼ [12¼, 12½] in), ending on a p row.
Follow graph for Labradoodle.
Row 1: K57 [60, 63] mc, k3ow, k44 [47, 50] mc.
Continue graph pattern until dog is finished.

FINISHING DETAILS
Eyes: With bl, Swiss darn 1 st for each eye.

JACK RUSSELL

MATERIALS

- Main colour: Cascade 220 in 8010 Natural – cream (mc); see jumper pattern for quantity
- Contrast colour: 50g (2oz) of Cascade 220 Heathers in 8400 Charcoal Grey (gr)
- 15g (½oz) of Cascade 220 in 8010 Natural – cream (cr)
- 10g (¼oz) of Cascade 220 in 8013 Walnut Heather – fawn (fn)
- Tiny amount of Cascade 220 in 8555 Black (bl) for eyes and nose

GRAPH

See page 124

WOMAN'S RAGLAN JUMPER (PAGE 16)

Our Jack Russell is knitted on a contrast square. Continue in st st until front measures 21 [22, 22] cm (8¼ [8¾, 8¾] in), ending on a p row.
NOTE: For version without a contrast square, work all gr sts in mc.
Row 1: K21 [23, 25] mc, k48gr, k21 [23, 25] mc.
Work 5 rows st st, colours as set. Then follow graph for Jack Russell.
Row 7: K21 [23, 25] mc, k11gr, k2cr, k17gr, k2cr, k16gr, k21 [23, 25] mc.
Continue graph pattern until dog is finished.
Work 6 rows to match bottom of square, ending on a k row.
Continue in mc.

WOMAN'S LONG AND LOOSE JUMPER (PAGE 18)

This is an example for knitting the Jack Russell without a square.
Continue in st st until front measures 33 [34, 35] cm (13 [13½, 13¾] in), ending on a p row.
Follow graph for Jack Russell.
Row 1: K40 [44, 48] mc, k2cr, k17mc, k2cr, k45 [49, 53] mc.
Continue graph pattern until dog is finished.

MAN'S JUMPER (PAGE 20)

This is an example for knitting the Jack Russell without a square.
Continue in st st until front measures 34 [35, 35] cm (13½ [13¾, 13¾] in), ending on a p row.
Follow graph for Jack Russell.
Row 1: K39 [42, 45] mc, k2cr, k17mc, k2cr, k44 [47, 50] mc.
Continue graph pattern until dog is finished.

FINISHING DETAILS

Eye: With bl, make a 3-loop French knot for eye.

MINIATURE SCHNAUZER

MATERIALS
- Main colour: Debbie Bliss Luxury Tweed Aran in 53 Meadow (mc); see jumper pattern for quantity
- 15g (½oz) of Rowan Kidsilk Haze in 00634 Cream (mohair – mo) – use FOUR strands together throughout
- 15g (½oz) of Cascade 220 Heathers in 8400 Charcoal Grey (gr)
- 5g (⅛oz) of Cascade 220 in 8555 Black (bl)
- 2 black beads for eyes, plus sewing needle and black thread for sewing on

GRAPH
See page 126

WOMAN'S RAGLAN JUMPER (PAGE 16)
Continue in st st until front measures 19 [20, 20] cm (7½ [8, 8] in), ending on a p row.
Follow graph for Miniature Schnauzer.
Row 1: K46 [48, 50] mc, k5mo, k39 [41, 43] mc.
Continue graph pattern, working loopy st with mo for eyebrows, until dog is finished.

WOMAN'S LONG AND LOOSE JUMPER (PAGE 18)
Continue in st st until front measures 29 [30, 31] cm (11½ [11¾, 12¼] in), ending on a p row.
Follow graph for Miniature Schnauzer.
Row 1: K54 [58, 62] mc, k5mo, k47 [51, 55] mc.
Continue graph pattern, working loopy st with mo for eyebrows, until dog is finished.

MAN'S JUMPER (PAGE 20)
Continue in st st until front measures 29 [29, 30] cm (11½ [11½, 11¾] in), ending on a p row.
Follow graph for Miniature Schnauzer.
Row 1: K53 [56, 59] mc, k5mo, k46 [49, 52] mc.
Continue graph pattern, working loopy st with mo for eyebrows, until dog is finished.

FINISHING DETAILS
Eyes: Sew on bead for each eye.

LOOPY STITCH
On a knit row, knit one stitch as normal but leave the stitch on the left-hand needle. Bring the yarn from the back to the front between the two needles. Loop the yarn around the index finger of your left hand. Take the yarn between the two needles to the back of the work. Knit the stitch from the left-hand needle as normal. You now have two stitches on the right-hand needle and a loop between them. Pass the first stitch over the second stitch to trap the loop, which is now secure. On a purl row, take the loop to the RS of the knitting and work knit stitches in purl.

WHIPPET

MATERIALS
- Main colour: Debbie Bliss Luxury Tweed Aran in 49 Rose (mc); see jumper pattern for quantity
- Contrast colour: 60g (2¼oz) of Cascade 220 Heathers in 8400 Charcoal Grey (gr)
- 15g (½oz) of Cascade 220 in 8505 White (wh)
- 10g (¼oz) of Cascade 220 in 9499 Sand – fawn (fn)
- Tiny amount of Cascade 220 in 8555 Black (bl) for eye and nose

GRAPH
See page 128

WOMAN'S RAGLAN JUMPER (PAGE 16)
Our Whippet is knitted on a contrast square. Continue in st st until front measures 20 [21, 21] cm (8 [8¼, 8¼] in), ending on a p row.
NOTE: For version without a contrast square, work all gr sts in mc.
Row 1: K13 [15, 17] mc, k64gr, k13 [15, 17] mc.
Work 3 rows st st, colours as set. Then follow graph for Whippet.
Row 5: K13 [15, 17] mc, k14gr, k2wh, k1gr, k1wh, k20gr, k1wh, k1gr, k2wh, k22gr, k13 [15, 17] mc.
Continue graph pattern until dog is finished.
Work 4 rows to match bottom of square, ending on a p row.
Continue in main colour.

WOMAN'S LONG AND LOOSE JUMPER (PAGE 18)
This is an example for knitting the Whippet without a square.
Continue in st st until front measures 32 [32, 34] cm (12½, [12½, 13½] in), ending on a p row.
Follow graph for Whippet.
Row 1: K35 [39, 43] mc, k2wh, k1mc, k1wh, k20mc, k1wh, k1mc, k2wh, k43 [47, 51] mc.
Continue graph pattern until dog is finished.

MAN'S JUMPER (PAGE 20)
This is an example for knitting the Whippet without a square.
Continue in st st until front measures 32 [32, 33] cm (12½, [12½, 13] in), ending on a p row.
Follow graph for Whippet.
Row 1: K34 [37, 40] mc, k2wh, k1mc, k1wh, k20mc, k1wh, k1mc, k2wh, k42 [45, 48] mc.
Continue graph pattern until dog is finished.

FINISHING DETAILS
Eye: With bl, make a 3-loop French knot for eye.

BORDER TERRIER

MATERIALS

- Main colour: Cascade 220 Heathers in 8836 Stonewash – blue lovat (mc); see jumper pattern for quantity
- Contrast colour: 50g (2oz) of Cascade 220 Heathers in 9600 Antiqued Heather – buttermilk (bt)
- 15g (½oz) of Cascade 220 Heathers in 2440 Vinci – coffee (co)
- 10g (¼oz) of Cascade 220 Heathers in 4002 Jet – charcoal (ch)

GRAPH

See page 121

WOMAN'S RAGLAN JUMPER (PAGE 16)

This is an example for knitting the Border Terrier without a square. Continue in st st until front measures 21 [22, 22] cm (8¼ [8¾, 8¾] in), ending on a p row.
Follow graph for Border Terrier.
Row 1: K27 [29, 31] mc, k3co, k1mc, k2co, k19mc, k3co, k35 [37, 39] mc.
Continue graph pattern until dog is finished.

WOMAN'S LONG AND LOOSE JUMPER (PAGE 18)

Our Border Terrier is knitted on a contrast square. Continue in st st until front measures 31 [32, 33] cm (12¼ [12½, 13] in), ending on a p row.
NOTE: For version without a contrast square, work all bt sts in mc.
Row 1: K22 [26, 30] mc, k62bt, k22 [26, 30] mc.
Work 3 rows st st, colours as set.
Then follow graph for Border Terrier.
Row 5: K22 [26, 30] mc, k13bt, k3co, k1bt, k2co, k19bt, k3co, k21bt, k22 [26, 30] mc.
Continue graph pattern until dog is finished.
Work 4 rows to match bottom of square, ending on a p row.
Continue in mc.

MAN'S JUMPER (PAGE 20)

This is an example for knitting the Border Terrier without a square. Continue in st st until front measures 32 [32, 33] cm (12½ [12½, 13] in), ending on a p row.
Follow graph for Border Terrier.
Row 1: K34 [37, 40] mc, k3co, k1mc, k2co, k19mc, k3co, k42 [45, 48] mc.
Continue graph pattern until dog is finished.

BORDER COLLIE

MATERIALS
- Main colour: Cascade 220 Heathers in 9560 Liberty Heather – purple heather (mc); see jumper pattern for quantity
- Contrast edge: 10g (¼oz) of Cascade 220 Heathers in 9450 Smoke Heather – green heather (gh)
- 15g (½oz) of Cascade 220 in 8555 Black (bl)
- 15g (½oz) of Cascade 220 in 8505 White (wh)
- Black bead for eye, plus sewing needle and black thread for sewing on (optional)

GRAPH
See page 120

WOMAN'S RAGLAN JUMPER (PAGE 16)
Continue in st st until front measures 20 [21, 21] cm (8 [8¼, 8¼] in), ending on a p row.
Follow graph for Border Collie.
Row 1: K34 [36, 38] mc, k2bl, k22mc, k3wh, k29 [31, 33] mc.
Continue graph pattern until dog is finished.

WOMAN'S LONG AND LOOSE JUMPER (PAGE 18)
Continue in st st until front measures 27 [28, 29] cm (10¾ [11, 11½] in), ending on a p row.
Follow graph for Border Collie.
Row 1: K37 [41, 45] mc, k2bl, k22mc, k3wh, k42 [46, 50] mc.
Continue graph pattern until dog is finished.

MAN'S JUMPER (PAGE 20)
Continue in st st until front measures 31 [31, 32] cm (12¼ [12¼, 12½] in), ending on a p row.
Follow graph for Border Collie.
Row 1: K36 [39, 42] mc, k2bl, k22mc, k3wh, k41 [44, 47] mc.
Continue graph pattern until dog is finished.

FINISHING DETAILS
Eye: Sew on black bead for eye.

WEST HIGHLAND TERRIER

MATERIALS
- Main colour: Cascade 220 in 9567 Smoky Blue – sage (mc); see jumper pattern for quantity
- 20g (¾oz) of Rowan Kidsilk Haze in 00634 Cream (mohair – mo) – use FOUR strands together throughout
- Tiny amount of Cascade 220 in 4192 Soft Pink (pk) for ears
- Tiny amount of Cascade 220 in 8555 Black (bl) for eye and nose
- Small amount of aran-weight yarn for collar
- Pair of 4mm (US 6) knitting needles for collar

GRAPH
See page 128

WOMAN'S RAGLAN JUMPER (PAGE 16)
Continue in st st until front measures 23 [24, 24] cm (9 [9½, 9½] in), ending on a p row.
Follow graph for West Highland Terrier.
Row 1: K28 [30, 32] mc, k3mo, k1mc, k1mo, k16mc, k1mo, k1mc, k3mo, k36 [38, 40] mc.
Continue graph pattern until dog is finished.

WOMAN'S LONG AND LOOSE JUMPER (PAGE 18)
Continue in st st until front measures 33 [34, 35] cm (13 [13½, 13¾] in), ending on a p row.
Follow graph for West Highland Terrier.
Row 1: K36 [40, 44] mc, k3mo, k1mc, k1mo, k16mc, k1mo, k1mc, k3mo, k44 [48, 52] mc.
Continue graph pattern until dog is finished.

MAN'S JUMPER (PAGE 20)
Continue in st st until front measures 33 [33, 34] cm (13 [13, 13½] in), ending on a p row.
Follow graph for West Highland Terrier.
Row 1: K35 [38, 41] mc, k3mo, k1mc, k1mo, k16mc, k1mo, k1mc, k3mo, k43 [46, 49] mc.
Continue graph pattern until dog is finished.

FINISHING DETAILS
Eye: With bl, make a 3-loop French knot for eye.
Collar: With 4mm (US 6) needles and collar colour, cast on 28 sts and knit 2 rows. Cast off. Push each end into the side of the dog's neck, and sew collar ends together on reverse side of jumper.

DACHSHUND

MATERIALS
- Main colour: Cascade 220 Heathers in 8401 Silver Grey (mc); see jumper pattern for quantity
- 15g (½oz) of Cascade 220 in 8555 Black (bl)
- 5g (⅛oz) of Cascade 220 in 2415 Sunflower – gold (gd)

GRAPH
See page 122

WOMAN'S RAGLAN JUMPER (PAGE 16)
Continue in st st until front measures 26 [27, 27] cm (10¼ [10¾, 10¾] in), ending on a p row.
Follow graph for Dachshund.
Row 1: K26 [28, 30] mc, k3gd, k27mc, k3gd, k31 [33, 35] mc.
Continue graph pattern until dog is finished.

WOMAN'S LONG AND LOOSE JUMPER (PAGE 18)
Continue in st st until front measures 37 [39, 41] cm (14½ [15¼, 16] in), ending on a p row.
Follow graph for Dachshund.
Row 1: K34 [38, 42] mc, k3gd, k27mc, k3gd, k39 [43, 47] mc.
Continue graph pattern until dog is finished.

MAN'S JUMPER (PAGE 20)
Continue in st st until front measures 37 [37, 39] cm (14½ [14½, 15¼] in), ending on a p row.
Follow graph for Dachshund.
Row 1: K33 [36, 39] mc, k3gd, k27mc, k3gd, k38 [41, 44] mc.
Continue graph pattern until dog is finished.

CAVE CANEM
(BEWARE OF THE DOG)

MATERIALS
- Main colour: Cascade 220 in 8555 Black (mc); see jumper pattern for quantity
- Contrast colour: 15g (½oz) of Cascade 220 in 8505 White (wh)

NOTE: Use separate balls of contrast yarn for each letter. Take the main colour across the back of each letter, weaving in when necessary (generally when carried over more than 3 stitches). Be careful not to pull the main colour too tight or the knitting will pucker.

GRAPH
See page 129

WOMAN'S RAGLAN JUMPER (PAGE 16)
Continue in st st until front measures 25 [26, 26] cm (10 [10¼, 10¼] in), ending on a p row.
Follow graph pattern for lettering.
Row 1: K16 [18, 20] mc, k2wh, k9mc, k2wh, k1mc, k9wh, k1mc, k2wh, k6mc, k2wh, k1mc, k2wh, k9mc, k2wh, k3mc, k3wh, k20 [22, 24] mc.
Continue graph pattern until lettering is finished.

WOMAN'S LONG AND LOOSE JUMPER (PAGE 18)
Continue in st st until front measures 34 [35, 36] cm (13½ [13¾, 14¼] in), ending on a p row.
Follow graph for lettering.
Row 1: K24 [28, 32] mc, k2wh, k9mc, k2wh, k1mc, k9wh, k1mc, k2wh, k6mc, k2wh, k1mc, k2wh, k9mc, k2wh, k3mc, k3wh, k28 [32, 36] mc.
Continue graph pattern until lettering is finished.

MAN'S JUMPER (PAGE 20)
Continue in st st until front measures 34 [34, 35] cm (13½ [13½, 13¾] in), ending on a p row.
Follow graph for lettering.
Row 1: K23 [26, 29] mc, k2wh, k9mc, k2wh, k1mc, k9wh, k1mc, k2wh, k6mc, k2wh, k1mc, k2wh, k9mc, k2wh, k3mc, k3wh, k27 [30, 33] mc.
Continue graph pattern until lettering is finished.

CHILD AND BABY
JUMPERS AND CARDIGANS

We have one Child's Jumper shape, which is round-neck, with dropped
shoulders, loose-fitting, and sized for ages 3–5, 5–7 and 7–9 years.
The Baby's Raglan Jumper is in a round-neck, raglan, sweatshirt
shape and is sized for ages 6–12 months, 1–2 years and 2–3 years.
The Baby's Cardigan is round-neck, with set-in sleeves and pockets,
and is sized for ages 0–3 months and 3–6 months. We have scaled down
a selection of the adult-size dog charts for the child and baby jumpers.
There are eight different dogs; all eight breeds are pictured on pages
76–79 to help you make your selection. The simplest are the Labrador
and West Highland Terrier. For a quick knit, we recommend the Baby's
Raglan Jumper: the perfect present for a dog-loving new parent.

CHILD'S JUMPER

MEASUREMENTS

Small
To fit age: 3–5 years
Chest flat: 34cm (13½in)
Length: 38cm (15in)

Medium
To fit age: 5–7 years
Chest flat: 36cm (14¼in)
Length: 43cm (17in)

Large
To fit age: 7–9 years
Chest flat: 39cm (15¼in)
Length: 49cm (19¼in))

MATERIALS

- Pair of 3.25mm (US 3) knitting needles
- Pair of 4mm (US 6) knitting needles
- Main colour (mc): Erika Knight British Blue Wool or Erika Knight British Blue 100

Size	Small	Medium	Large
Quantity	200g (7oz)	230g (8oz)	280g (10oz)

- 10g (¼oz) of Erika Knight yarn in contrast colour (optional)

TENSION
22 sts and 30 rows to 10cm (4in) measured over st st using 4mm (US 6) needles

DOG ON FRONT
All of the dogs are different shapes and colours. For yarn requirements and knitting instructions, refer to the index of dogs on page 140. This will direct you to the instructions and graph for your chosen breed.

BACK
With 3.25mm (US 3) needles and mc, cast on 76 [82, 88] sts.
Work 10 rows k1, p1 rib.
NOTE: For version with contrast edge, use contrast yarn to cast on and work first rib row, then change to mc to complete rib.
Change to 4mm (US 6) needles.
Beg with a k row, continue in st st until back measures 23 [28, 33] cm (9 [11, 13] in), ending on a p row.
SHAPE ARMHOLES:
Cast off 6 [7, 8] sts at beg of next 2 rows. *(64 [68, 72] sts)*
Continue straight until armhole measures 14 [14, 15] cm (5½ [5½, 6] in), ending on a p row.

SHAPE SHOULDERS:
Next row (RS): Cast off 6 [6, 7] sts, k14 [15, 16] including st used to cast off, turn, leaving rem sts on a holder. Work each side separately:
Next row (WS): Dec 1 st at neck edge, p to end.
Next row (RS): Cast off 6 [6, 7] sts, k to end.
Next row (WS): Dec 1 st at neck edge, p to end.
Next row (RS): Cast off rem 6 [7, 7] sts.
With RS facing, slip centre 24 [26, 26] sts onto a holder for neck edge, rejoin yarn and complete to match first side, reversing shaping.

FRONT
Work as for back to armhole shaping, positioning and knitting the dog as instructed for your chosen dog breed (see index of dogs, page 140).
SHAPE ARMHOLES:
Cast off 6 [7, 8] sts at beg of next 2 rows. *(64 [68, 72] sts)*
Continue straight until armhole measures 5 [5, 6] cm (2 [2, 2¼] in), ending on a p row.
SHAPE FRONT NECK:
With RS facing, k25 [26, 28], turn, leaving rem sts on a holder.
Work each side separately:
Dec 1 st at neck edge of every row 4 times, and then at neck edge of every other row 3 times. *(18 [19, 21] sts)*

Continue straight until front matches back at shoulder, ending on a p row.

SHAPE SHOULDERS:

Next row (RS): Cast off 6 [6, 7] sts, k to end.

Next row (WS): Purl.

Next row (RS): Cast off 6 [6, 7] sts.

Next row (WS): Purl.

Next row (RS): Cast off rem 6 [7, 7] sts.

With RS facing, slip centre 14 [16, 16] sts onto a holder, rejoin yarn and k to end. Complete to match first side, reversing shaping.

SLEEVES (MAKE 2)

With 3.25mm (US 3) needles, cast on 42 [44, 46] sts and work rib as for back. Change to 4mm (US 6) needles.

Beg with a k row, continue in st st, shaping sides by inc 1 st at each end of next and every following 6th row 12 [12, 10] times, and then at each end of every 8th row 0 [0, 3] times. *(66 [68, 72] sts)* Continue straight until sleeve measures 27 [30, 33] cm (10¾ [11¾, 13] in), ending on a p row. Cast off 6 [7, 8] sts at beg of next 2 rows. *(54 [54, 56] sts)* Cast off rem sts.

MAKING UP

Block each piece and, using a warm iron and cloth, press all parts except ribbing. Sew in ends. Using backstitch or mattress stitch, sew right shoulder together.

NECK EDGE

With 3.25mm (US 3) needles and mc and RS facing, starting at left front shoulder pick up 17 [17, 19] sts down left front neck shaping, 14 [16, 16] sts across centre front, 17 [17, 19] sts up right front neck shaping, 5 sts down right back shaping, 34 [36, 36] sts across back neck and 5 sts up left back shaping. *(82 [86, 90] sts)* Work 6 rows k1, p1 rib. Cast off loosely in rib.

TO FINISH

Using backstitch or mattress stitch, sew left shoulder together and neck edge. Set in sleeves and sew up side and sleeve seams. Press with a damp cloth.

BABY'S RAGLAN JUMPER

MEASUREMENTS

Small
To fit age: 6–12 months
Chest flat: 25cm (10in)
To fit chest: 44cm (17¼in)
Length: 25cm (10in)

Medium
To fit age: 1–2 years
Chest flat: 28cm (11in)
To fit chest: 48cm (19in)
Length: 29cm (11½in)

Large
To fit age: 2–3 years
Chest flat: 31cm (12¼in)
To fit chest: 53cm (21in)
Length: 32cm (12½in)

MATERIALS

- Pair of 3.25mm (US 3) knitting needles
- Pair of 4mm (US 6) knitting needles
- Main colour (mc): Erika Knight British Blue Wool or Erika Knight British Blue 100

Size	Small	Medium	Large
Quantity	120g (4¼oz)	145g (5oz)	175g (6oz)

- 10g (¼oz) of Erika Knight yarn in contrast colour (optional)

TENSION
22 sts and 30 rows to 10cm (4in) measured over st st using 4mm (US 6) needles

DOG ON FRONT
All of the dogs are different shapes and colours. For yarn requirements and knitting instructions, refer to the index of dogs on page 140. This will direct you to the instructions and graph for your chosen breed.

BACK
With 3.25mm (US 3) needles and mc, cast on 58 [64, 70] sts.
Work 6 [6, 8] rows k1, p1 rib.
NOTE: For version with contrast edge, use contrast yarn to cast on and work first rib row, then change to mc to complete rib.
Change to 4mm (US 6) needles.
Beg with a k row, continue in st st until back measures 16.5 [18, 20] cm (6½ [7, 8] in), ending on a p row.
SHAPE ARMHOLES:
Cast off 4 [4, 5] sts at beg of next 2 rows. *(50 [56, 60] sts)*
Dec 1 st at each end of next and every other row 13 [16, 17] times, ending on a p row. *(24 [24, 26] sts)*

Leave rem 24 [24, 26] sts on a holder for neck edge.

FRONT
Work as for back to armhole shaping, positioning and knitting the dog as instructed for your chosen dog breed (see index of dogs, page 140).
SHAPE ARMHOLES:
Cast off 4 [4, 5] sts at beg of next 2 rows. *(50 [56, 60] sts)*
Dec 1 st at each end of next and every other row 8 [10, 11] times, ending on a p row. *(34 [36, 38] sts)*
SHAPE FRONT NECK:
With RS facing, k2tog, k9 [10, 11], turn, leaving rem sts on a holder.
Work each side separately:

Dec 1 st at neck edge of next 2 rows, and then at neck edge of every other row 2 [2, 3] times, and **at the same time** continue raglan shaping by dec 1 st at armhole edge of every other row until 2 sts remain, ending on a p row, then k2tog and fasten off.
With RS facing, slip centre 12 sts onto a holder for neck edge, rejoin yarn and k to last 2 sts, k2tog.
Complete to match first side, reversing shaping.

SLEEVES (MAKE 2)

With 3.25mm (US 3) needles, cast on 34 [36, 40] sts and work rib as for back.

Change to 4mm (US 6) needles.

Next row (RS): K2, inc, k28 [30, 34], inc, k2. *(36 [38, 42] sts)*

Beg with a p row, continue in st st, shaping sides by inc 1 st as set at each end of every 8th [6th, 6th] row 5 [7, 7] times. *(46 [52, 56] sts)*

Continue straight until sleeve measures 18 [20, 22] cm (7 [8, 8¾] in), ending on a p row.

SHAPE SLEEVE TOP:

Cast off 4 [4, 5] sts at beg of next 2 rows. *(38 [44, 46] sts)*

Dec 1 st at each end of next and every other row 13 [16, 17] times, ending on a p row. *(12 sts)*

Leave rem 12 sts on a holder for neck edge.

MAKING UP

Block each piece and, using a warm iron and cloth, press all parts except ribbing. Sew in ends. Using backstitch or mattress stitch, sew up raglan seams but leave left back raglan open.

NECK EDGE

With 3.25mm (US 3) needles and mc and RS facing, pick up 12 sts across top of left sleeve, 11 [13, 14] sts down left front neck shaping, 12 sts across centre front, 11 [13, 14] sts up right front neck shaping, 12 sts across top of right sleeve and 24 [24, 26] sts across back neck. *(82 [86, 90] sts)*

Work 5 rows k1, p1 rib.

Cast off loosely in rib.

TO FINISH

Using backstitch or mattress stitch, sew up remaining raglan seam and neck edge. Sew up side and sleeve seams. Press with a damp cloth.

BABY'S CARDIGAN

MEASUREMENTS

Small
To fit age: 0–3 months
Chest flat: 19cm (7½in)
Length: 23cm (9in)

Medium
To fit age: 3–6 months
Chest flat: 22cm (8¾in)
Length: 26cm (10¼in)

MATERIALS

- Pair of 3.25mm (US 3) knitting needles
- Pair of 4mm (US 6) knitting needles
- Main colour (mc): Erika Knight British Blue Wool or Erika Knight British Blue 100

Size	Small	Medium
Quantity	90g (3¼oz)	110g (4oz)

- 10g (¼oz) of Erika Knight yarn in contrast colour (optional):
  Miniature Schnauzer: Mouse (grey – mu)
  Dachshund: Mrs Dalloway (ochre – oc)
  Jack Russell: Milk Chocolate (me)
- 6 [7] small buttons

TENSION

22 sts and 30 rows to 10cm (4in) measured over st st using 4mm (US 6) needles

DOGS ON FRONT

Erika Knight British Blue Wool or Erika Knight British Blue 100 in the following colours:
Miniature Schnauzer: 5g (⅛oz) of Mouse (grey – mu), 5g (⅛oz) of Pitch (black – bl), 5g (⅛oz) of Rowan Kidsilk Haze in 00634 Cream (mohair – mo) – use THREE strands of mo together throughout
Dachshund: 5g (⅛oz) of Pitch (black – bl), 5g (⅛oz) of Mrs Dalloway (ochre – oc)
Jack Russell: 5g (⅛oz) of Milk (cream – cr), 5g (⅛oz) of Milk Chocolate (me), small amount of Pitch (black – bl) for eye and nose. For picture see page 100.

GRAPHS

See page 136

NOTE: Work eyebrows of Miniature Schnauzer using THREE strands of mo together and loopy stitch (see page 75).

BACK

With 3.25mm (US 3) needles and mc, cast on 44 [50] sts.

Row 1 (RS): [K1, p1] to end.

Row 2: [P1, k1] to end.

These 2 rows set moss st.

Repeat rows 1–2 twice more.

(6 rows in total)

NOTE: For version with contrast edge, use contrast yarn to cast on and work first moss st row, then change to mc to complete hem.

Change to 4mm (US 6) needles.

Beg with a k row, continue in st st until back measures 12 [14] cm (4¾ [5½] in), ending on a p row.

SHAPE ARMHOLES:

Cast off 3 [4] sts at beg of next 2 rows, and then 1 st at each end of next and every other row 3 times. *(32 [36] sts)*

Continue straight until armhole measures 11 [12] cm (4¼ [4¾] in), ending on a p row.

SHAPE SHOULDERS:

Cast off 7 [8] sts at beg of next 2 rows. Leave rem 18 [20] sts on a holder for neck edge.

POCKET BACK (MAKE 2)

With 4mm (US 6) needles and mc, cast on 14 sts.

Beg with a k row, work 14 rows st st. Leave 14 sts on a holder.

LEFT FRONT

With 3.25mm (US 3) needles and mc, cast on 22 [24] sts and work 6 rows moss st as for back, inc 0 [1] st on last row. *(22 [25] sts)*

Change to 4mm (US 6) needles.

Beg with a k row, work 14 rows st st. Cut yarn.

Pocket top: Slip 4 [5] sts onto a holder, rejoin mc, then on next 14 sts only with 3.25mm (US 3) needles, work 3 rows moss st and then cast off.

With 4mm (US 6) needles and mc and beg with a k row, k4 [5] from holder, replace cast-off sts with 14 sts from pocket back and begin graph for your chosen dog as follows:

Jack Russell: K5mc, k2cr, k7mc, continue in mc and k4 [6].

Miniature Schnauzer: K5mc, k4mu, k5mc, continue in mc and k4 [6].

Dachshund: K2mc, k2bl, k1mc, k2bl, k7mc, continue in mc and k4 [6].

Continue graph pattern until dog is finished and then continue in mc and st st, and **at the same time** shape armhole when front measures 12 [14] cm (4¾ [5½] in), ending on a p row.

SHAPE ARMHOLE:

Cast off 3 [4] sts at beg of next row, then dec 1 st at armhole edge on every other row 3 times. *(16 [18] sts)*

Continue until armhole measures 6cm (2¼in), ending on a p row.

SHAPE FRONT NECK:

With RS facing, k12 [14], turn, leaving rem 4 sts on a holder.

Dec 1 st at neck edge of every row 3 [4] times, and then at neck edge of every other row twice. *(7 [8] sts)*

Continue straight until armhole measures 11 [12] cm (4¼ [4¾] in), ending on a p row.

Cast off.

RIGHT FRONT

Work as for left front to pocket top.

Pocket top: Slip 4 [6] sts onto a holder, rejoin mc, then on next 14 sts only with 3.25mm (US 3) needles, work 3 rows moss st and then cast off.

With 4mm (US 6) needles and mc and beg with a k row, k4 [6] from holder, replace cast-off sts with 14 sts from pocket back and begin graph for your chosen dog as follows:

Jack Russell: K7mc, k2cr, k5mc, continue in mc and k4 [5].

Miniature Schnauzer: K5mc, k4mu, k5mc, continue in mc and k4 [5].

Dachshund: K7mc, k2bl, k1mc, k2bl, k2mc, continue in mc and k4 [5].

Continue graph pattern until dog is finished and then continue in mc and st st, and **at the same time** shape armhole when front measures 12 [14] cm (4¾ [5½] in), ending on a k row.

SHAPE ARMHOLE:

Cast off 3 [4] sts at beg of next row, then dec 1 st at armhole edge of next and every other row 3 times. *(16 [18] sts)*

Continue until armhole measures 6cm (2¼in), ending on a p row.

SHAPE FRONT NECK:

With RS facing, k4, leave these 4 sts on a holder, k to end. (12 [14] sts)
Dec 1 st at neck edge of every row 3 [4] times, and then at neck edge of every other row twice. (7 [8] sts)
Continue straight until armhole measures 11 [12] cm (4¼ [4¾] in), ending on a k row.
Cast off.

SLEEVES (MAKE 2)

With 3.25mm (US 3) needles, cast on 28 [32] sts and work 6 rows moss st as for back.
Change to 4mm (US 6) needles.
Next row (RS): K2, inc, k22 [26], inc, k2. (30 [34] sts)
Beg with a p row, continue in st st, shaping sides by inc 1 st as set at each end of every 6th row twice, and then at each end of every 8th row twice. (38 [42] sts)
Continue straight until sleeve measures 15 [16] cm (6 [6¼] in), ending on a p row.

SHAPE SLEEVE TOP:

Cast off 3 [4] sts at beg of next 2 rows, and then 1 st at each end of next and every other row 3 times, ending on a p row. (26 [28] sts)
Cast off.

MAKING UP

Block each piece and, using a warm iron and cloth, press all parts except ribbing. Sew in ends. Using backstitch or mattress stitch, sew shoulders together.

NECK EDGE

With 3.25mm (US 3) needles and RS facing, skip 4 sts from stitch holder, rejoin mc and pick up 12 [14] sts from right front neck shaping, 18 [20] sts across back neck, 12 [14] sts from left front neck shaping and 4 sts from stitch holder. (50 [56] sts)
Work 5 rows moss st.
NOTE: For version with contrast edge, change to contrast colour for final row.
Cast off in moss st.

LEFT BUTTONBAND

With 3.25mm (US 3) needles and mc and RS facing, starting at neck edge pick up 50 [54] sts along left side of front.
Starting at hem with a WS row, work 4 rows moss st.
NOTE: For version with contrast edge, use contrast colour for 2 sts at neck hem edge on each row of buttonband.
Cast off in moss st.

RIGHT BUTTONBAND

Work to match left buttonband but work row 2 as follows to add buttonholes:
Row 2 (small size only): K1, p1, *k2tog, yo, [k1, p1] 3 times, k1, p2tog, yo, [p1, k1] 3 times, p1; repeat from * once more, k2tog, yo, [k1, p1] 3 times, k2tog, yo, [k1, p1].
Row 2 (medium size only): K1, p1, *k2tog, yo, [k1, p1] 3 times; repeat from * 3 times more, k1, p2tog, yo, [p1, k1] 3 times, p1, k2tog, yo, [k1, p1] twice, k2tog, yo, k1, p1.

TO FINISH

Using backstitch or mattress stitch, set in sleeves and sew up side and sleeve seams. Press with a damp cloth. Sew on buttons.
Eyes: With bl, make a 3-loop French knot for each eye.
Nose: With bl, Swiss darn 1 st for nose.

LOOPY STITCH

The Miniature Schnauzer's eyebrows are worked in loopy stitch. On a knit row, knit one stitch as normal but leave the stitch on the left-hand needle. Bring the yarn from the back to the front between the two needles. Loop the yarn around the index finger of your left hand. Take the yarn between the two needles to the back of the work. Knit the stitch from the left-hand needle as normal. You now have two stitches on the right-hand needle and a loop between them. Pass the first stitch over the second stitch to trap the loop, which is now secure. On a purl row, take the loop to the RS of the knitting and work knit stitches in purl.

West Highland Terrier

PAGE 80

Dalmatian

PAGE 82

Labrador

PAGE 84

Dachshund

PAGE 86

Pug
PAGE 88

Border Collie
PAGE 90

Jack Russell

PAGE 92

Whippet

PAGE 94

WEST HIGHLAND TERRIER

MATERIALS

- Main colour: Erika Knight British Blue Wool in Pretty – pale pink (mc)
- 15g (½oz) of Rowan Kidsilk Haze in Cream (mohair – mo) – use THREE strands together throughout
- Tiny amount of Erika Knight British Blue Wool in Pitch – black (bl) for nose and eye
- Small amount of Erika Knight British Blue Wool in French – mauve (fr) for collar

GRAPH

See page 135

BABY'S RAGLAN JUMPER (PAGE 70)

Continue in st st until front measures 8 [10, 13] cm (3 [4, 5] in), ending on a p row.

Follow graph for West Highland Terrier.

Row 1: K15 [18, 21] mc, k4mo, k14mc, k3mo, k22 [25, 28] mc.

Continue graph pattern until dog is finished.

CHILD'S JUMPER (PAGE 68)

Continue in st st until front measures 15 [18, 22] cm (6 [7, 8¾] in), ending on a p row.

Follow graph for West Highland Terrier.

Row 1: K24 [27, 30] mc, k4mo, k14mc, k3mo, k31 [34, 37] mc.

Continue graph pattern until dog is finished.

FINISHING DETAILS

Eye: With bl, make a 3-loop French knot for eye.

Collar: With 4mm (US 6) needles and fr, cast on 20 sts and knit 1 row. Cast off. Push each end into the side of the dog's neck, and sew collar ends together on reverse side of jumper.

DALMATIAN

MATERIALS

- Main colour: Erika Knight British Blue 100 in Ballet Russes – bright pink (mc)
- 10g (¼oz) of Erika Knight British Blue Wool in Milk – cream (cr)
- 5g (⅛oz) of Erika Knight British Blue Wool in Pitch – black (bl)

GRAPH

See page 133

BABY'S RAGLAN JUMPER (PAGE 70)

Continue in st st until front measures 8 [11, 14] cm (3 [4¼, 5½] in), ending on a p row.
Follow graph for Dalmatian.
Row 1: K19 [22, 25] mc, k2cr, k17mc, k2cr, k18 [21, 24] mc.
Continue graph pattern until dog is finished.

CHILD'S JUMPER (PAGE 68)

Continue in st st until front measures 14 [18, 22] cm (5½ [7, 8¾] in), ending on a p row.
Follow graph for Dalmatian.
Row 1: K28 [31, 34] mc, k2cr, k17mc, k2cr, k27 [30, 33] mc.
Continue graph pattern until dog is finished.

LABRADOR

MATERIALS

- Main colour: Erika Knight British Blue Wool in Milk – cream (mc)
- 10g (¼oz) of Erika Knight British Blue Wool in Pitch – black (bl)
- Small amount of DK-weight yarn in brown (br) for eye

GRAPH
See page 134

BABY'S RAGLAN JUMPER (PAGE 70)
Continue in st st until front measures 8 [11, 14] cm (3 [4¼, 5½] in), ending on a p row.
Follow graph for Labrador.
Row 1: K19 [22, 25] mc, k2bl, k17mc, k2bl, k18 [21, 24] mc.
Continue graph pattern until dog is finished.

CHILD'S JUMPER (PAGE 68)
Continue in st st until front measures 14 [18, 22] cm (5½ [7, 8¾] in), ending on a p row.
Follow graph for Labrador.
Row 1: K28 [31, 34] mc, k2bl, k17mc, k2bl, k27 [30, 33] mc.
Continue graph pattern until dog is finished.

FINISHING DETAILS
Eye: With br, make a 3-loop French knot for eye.

DACHSHUND

MATERIALS
- Main colour: Erika Knight British Blue 100 in French – mauve (mc)
- Contrast stripe: 20g (¾oz) of Erika Knight British Blue Wool in Milk – cream (cr)
- 10g (¼oz) of Erika Knight British Blue Wool in Pitch – black (bl)
- 5g (⅛oz) of Erika Knight British Blue 100 in Mrs Dalloway – ochre (oc)
- Black bead for eye, plus sewing needle and black thread for sewing on (optional)

GRAPH
See page 132

CHILD'S JUMPER
(PAGE 68)
Because of its length, the Dachshund is suitable for a child-size jumper only. Our Dachshund is knitted on a contrast stripe. Continue in st st until front measures 21 [26, 31] cm (8¼ [10¼, 12¼] in), ending on a p row.
NOTE: For version without a contrast stripe, work first and last bl rows and all cr sts in mc.
START STRIPE:
Work 1 row in bl and then 3 rows in cr, ending on a p row.
Follow graph for Dachshund.
Row 5: K24 [27, 30] cr, k1bl, k1oc, k21cr, k1bl, k1oc, k27 [30, 33] cr.
Continue graph pattern until dog is finished, ending on a k row.
Work 3 rows in cr and then 1 row in bl, ending on a k row.
Continue in mc.

FINISHING DETAILS
Eye: Sew on bead for eye, just below eyebrow stitch (optional).

PUG

MATERIALS
- Main colour: Erika Knight British Blue Wool in Mr Bhasin – petrol (mc)
- 10g (¼oz) of Erika Knight British Blue Wool in Fawn (fn)
- 5g (⅛oz) of Erika Knight British Blue Wool in Pitch – black (bl)
- Tiny amount of Erika Knight British Blue Wool in Milk – cream (cr) for eye

GRAPH
See page 134

BABY'S RAGLAN JUMPER (PAGE 70)
Continue in st st until front measures 9 [11, 14] cm (3½ [4¼, 5½] in), ending on a p row.
Follow graph for Pug.
Row 1: K17 [20, 23] mc, k3fn, k12mc, k3fn, k23 [26, 29] mc.
Continue graph pattern until dog is finished.

CHILD'S JUMPER (PAGE 68)
Continue in st st until front measures 15 [18, 22] cm (6 [7, 8¾] in), ending on a p row.
Follow graph for Pug.
Row 1: K26 [29, 32] mc, k3fn, k12mc, k3fn, k32 [35, 38] mc.
Continue graph pattern until dog is finished.

FINISHING DETAILS
Eyes: With bl, make a 3-loop French knot for each eye and sew a small slanting stitch above each eye in cr.

BORDER COLLIE

MATERIALS
- Main colour: Erika Knight British Blue Wool in Iced Gem – aqua (mc)
- 10g (¼oz) of Erika Knight British Blue Wool in Milk – cream (cr)
- 10g (¼oz) of Erika Knight British Blue Wool in Pitch – black (bl)
- Black bead for eye, plus sewing needle and black thread for sewing on (optional – child's jumper only)

GRAPH
See page 132

BABY'S RAGLAN JUMPER (PAGE 70)
Continue in st st until front measures 8 [11, 14] cm (3 [4¼, 5½] in), ending on a p row.
Follow graph for Border Collie.
Row 1: K19 [22, 25] mc, k3bl, k14mc, k2cr, k20 [23, 26] mc.
Continue graph pattern until dog is finished.

CHILD'S JUMPER (PAGE 68)
Continue in st st until front measures 15 [18, 22] cm (6 [7, 8¾] in), ending on a p row.
Follow graph for Border Collie.
Row 1: K28 [31, 34] mc, k2bl, k14mc, k3cr, k29 [32, 35] mc.
Continue graph pattern until dog is finished.

FINISHING DETAILS
Eye: On child's jumper only, sew on bead for eye (optional).

JACK RUSSELL

MATERIALS

- Main colour: Erika Knight British Blue Wool in Mouse – grey (mc)
- Contrast colour (child's jumper only): 20g (¾oz) of Erika Knight British Blue 100 in Kanoko – pale blue (pb)
- 10g (¼oz) of Erika Knight British Blue Wool in Milk – cream (cr)
- 5g (⅛oz) of Erika Knight British Blue Wool in Milk Chocolate (me)
- Small amount of Erika Knight British Blue Wool in 4002 Pitch – black (bl) for eye and nose

GRAPH

See page 133

BABY'S RAGLAN JUMPER (PAGE 70)

This is an example for knitting the Jack Russell without an oval.

Continue in st st until front measures 8 [11, 14] cm (3 [4¼, 5½] in), ending on a p row.

Follow graph for Jack Russell.

Row 1: K19 [22, 25] mc, k2cr, k17mc, k2cr, k18 [21, 24] mc.

Continue graph pattern until dog is finished.

CHILD'S JUMPER (PAGE 68)

Our Jack Russell is knitted on a contrast oval. Continue in st st until front measures 12 [16, 20] cm (4¾ [6¼, 8] in), ending on a p row.

NOTE: For version without a contrast oval, work all pb sts in mc.

Follow graph for Jack Russell in oval.

Row 1: K34 [37, 40] mc, k8pb, k34 [37, 40] mc.

Continue to follow graph for oval.

START OF JACK RUSSELL:

Row 7: K22 [25, 28] mc, k4pb, k2cr, k17pb, k2cr, k7pb, k22 [25, 28] mc.

Continue graph pattern until dog and oval are finished.

Continue in mc.

FINISHING DETAILS

Eye: With bl, make a 3-loop French knot for eye.

Nose: With bl, Swiss darn 1 st for nose.

WHIPPET

MATERIALS
- Main colour: Erika Knight British Blue 100 in Kanoko – pale blue (mc)
- 10g (¼oz) of Erika Knight British Blue Wool in Milk – cream (cr)
- 5g (⅛oz) of Erika Knight British Blue Wool in Mouse – grey (mu)
- Tiny amount of Erika Knight British Blue Wool in Pitch – black (bl) for nose and eye

GRAPH
See page 135

BABY'S RAGLAN JUMPER
(PAGE 70)
Continue in st st until front measures 7 [10, 13] cm (2¾ [4, 5] in), ending on a p row.
Follow graph for Whippet.
Row 1: K17 [20, 23] mc, k2cr, k17mc, k2cr, k20 [23, 26] mc.
Continue graph pattern until dog is finished.

CHILD'S JUMPER
(PAGE 68)
Continue in st st until front measures 14 [18, 22] cm (5½ [7, 8¾] in), ending on a p row.
Follow graph for Whippet.
Row 1: K26 [29, 32] mc, k2cr, k17mc, k2cr, k29 [32, 35] mc.
Continue graph pattern until dog is finished.

FINISHING DETAILS
Eye: With bl, make a 3-loop French knot for eye.

ACCESSORIES

We have included a mixture of adult, child and dog accessories; all of the accessories are pictured on pages 98–99 to help you make your selection. The Pug Hat and Jack Russell Scarf are both for adults. If you want, you can choose another dog breed – most of the graphs will fit (the index of dogs on page 140 lists the stitch and row dimensions of each dog breed). The adorable Pug, Jack Russell and Dachshund Boots are for babies aged 3–6 months. The spectacular Dalmatian Onesie is for babies aged 3–6 months and 6–12 months. The Patchwork Baby Blanket can be customised to suit the child, and is the perfect present to hand down from generation to generation. The Dog Coat is knitted in aran-weight yarn. All the adult jumpers are also knitted in aran yarn, so you and your dog can complement one another.

Pug hat

PAGE 100

Dalmatian onesie

PAGE 102

Dachshund boots

PAGE 106

Pug boots

PAGE 108

Jack Russell boots

PAGE 111

Jack Russell scarf

PAGE 110

Patchwork baby blanket

PAGE 114

Dog coat

PAGE 112

PUG HAT

MEASUREMENTS
To fit average-size adult head
Length: 30cm (11¾in)

MATERIALS
- Pair of 3.25mm (US 3) knitting needles
- Pair of 4mm (US 6) knitting needles
- 80g (2¾oz) of Erika Knight British Blue Wool in French – mauve (mc)
- 15g (½oz) of Erika Knight British Blue Wool in Fawn (fn)
- Tiny amount of Erika Knight British Blue Wool in Pitch – black (bl)

TENSION
11 sts and 15 rows to 5cm (2in) measured over st st using 4mm (US 6) needles

GRAPH
See page 134 for Pug (child size)

HAT
With 3.25mm (US 3) needles and mc, cast on 108 sts.
Work k2, p2 rib for 7cm (2¾in).
Change to 4mm (US 6) needles.
Beg with a k row, continue in st st until work measures 12cm (4¾in), ending on a p row.
Follow graph for Pug, placing dog in centre of hat.
Row 1 of dog: K48mc, k3fn, k12mc, k3fn, k42mc.
Continue graph pattern until dog is finished and work measures 28cm (11in), ending on a p row.

SHAPE TOP OF HAT:
Next row: K2tog, [k10, k2tog] 8 times, k8, k2tog. *(98 sts)*
Next row: Purl.
Next row: K2tog, [k9, k2tog] 8 times, k6, k2tog. *(88 sts)*
Next row: Purl.
Next row: K2tog, [k8, k2tog] 8 times, k4, k2tog. *(78 sts)*
Next row: Purl.
Next row: K2tog, [k7, k2tog] 8 times, k2, k2tog. *(68 sts)*
Next row: Purl.
Next row: K2tog, [k6, k2tog] 8 times, k2. *(59 sts)*
Next row: Purl.
Cast off.

MAKING UP
Sew up side seam using mattress stitch for rib and whipstitch for remainder. Sew in ends.

DALMATIAN ONESIE

MEASUREMENTS

Small
To fit age: 3–6 months
Length to shoulder: 56cm (22in)
Chest flat: 33cm (13in)
Sleeves to armpit: 16cm (6¼in)

Medium
To fit age: 6–12 months
Length to shoulder: 60cm (23½in)
Chest flat: 38cm (15in)
Sleeves to armpit: 18cm (7in)

MATERIALS

• Pair of 4mm (US 6) knitting needles
• Pair of 5mm (US 8) knitting needles
• Cascade 220 Aran in 8505 White (wh)

Size	Small	Medium
Quantity	325g (11½oz)	350g (12½oz)

• 50g (2oz) of Cascade 220 Aran in 8555 Black (bl)
• 6 black buttons

TENSION
18 sts and 24 rows to 10cm (4in) measured over st st using
5mm (US 8) needles

GRAPHS
See pages 137 and 138

NOTE: Work odd-numbered rows on the graphs as knit (read from right to left) and even-numbered rows as purl (read from left to right). Use the Fair Isle method (see page 9) for working Dalmatian spots over the whole of the st st sections of the legs, body, hood and sleeves of the onesie.

LEGS (MAKE 4 PIECES)

Left back leg: With 4mm (US 6) needles and wh, cast on 18 [20] sts. Work 10 rows k1, p1 rib.

Change to 5mm (US 8) needles.

Beg with a k row and working spot pattern from graph 1, continue in st st.

Work 34 [40] rows, inc 1 st on outer edge (beg) of every 8th [10th] row 4 [3] times, and **at the same time** inc 1 st on inside leg (end) of every 6th [4th] row 5 [7] times. (27 [30] sts) Leave rem sts on a holder for back.

Right front leg: Work as for left back leg.

Left front leg: Work as for left back leg but reverse shaping.

Right back leg: Work as for left back leg but reverse shaping.

NOTE: The increase on every 6th [4th] row should be on the inside of all four leg pieces.

BACK

With 5mm (US 8) needles and wh and RS facing, k27 [30] sts from holder for right back leg, then k27 [30] sts from holder for left back leg (inner leg increases should be in centre of this needle). (54 [60] sts)

Beg with a p row and continuing spot pattern from graph 2 row 2, continue in st st.

Inc 1 st at each end of every following 8th [10th] row from previous inc 4 [5] times. (62 [70] sts)

Continue straight until back measures 40 [43] cm (15¾ [17] in), ending on a p row.

SHAPE ARMHOLES:

Cast off 3 sts at each end of next 2 rows, then dec 1 st at each end of next and every other row 4 [5] times. (48 [54] sts)

Continue straight until armhole measures 16 [17] cm (6¼ [6¾] in), ending on a k row.

Cast off 12 [14] sts, p24 [26] including st used to cast off, leave centre 24 [26] sts on a holder for back of hood, then cast off rem sts.

FRONT

With 5mm (US 8) needles and wh and RS facing, k27 [30] sts from holder for left front leg, then k27 [30] sts from holder for right front leg (inner leg increases should be in centre of this needle). (54 [60] sts)

Beg with a p row and continuing spot pattern from graph 2 row 2, work in st st for 3cm (1¼in), ending on a p row (there will be one inc at each end of one row in this section). (56 [62] sts)

DIVIDE FOR FRONT OPENING:

With RS facing, k26 [29], turn, leaving rem 30 [33] sts on a holder for right front.

Working on 26 [29] sts for left front, continue in st st, inc 1 st on outer edge of every 8th [10th] row 3 [4] times. (29 [33] sts)

Continue straight until left front measures 40 [43] cm (15¾ [17] in), ending on a p row.

SHAPE ARMHOLE:

Cast off 3 sts at beg of next row, and then 1 st at armhole edge of every other row 4 [5] times. (22 [25] sts)

Continue straight until armhole measures 12 [13] cm (4¾ [5] in), ending on a p row.

SHAPE FRONT NECK:

K17 [20], leaving rem 5 sts on holder for centre front neck.

Dec 1 st at neck edge of every row 3 [4] times, and then 1 st at neck edge of every other row twice. (12 [14] sts)

Continue until armhole measures 16 [17] cm (6¼ [6¾] in), ending on a p row.

Cast off for shoulder.

Working on 30 [33] sts from holder for right front, cast off 4 sts and then complete to match left front, reversing all shaping.

BACK AND TOP OF HOOD

With 5mm (US 8) needles and RS facing, rejoin yarns and pattern 24 [26] sts from holder for back of hood.

Beg with a p row and continuing spot pattern from graph 1, work in st st for 21 [23] cm (8¼ [9] in).

Leave sts on a holder for buttonband edging.

SIDES OF HOOD
(MAKE 2 PIECES)
Left side: With 5mm (US 8) needles
and wh, cast on 10 sts.
Beg with a k row and working spot
pattern from graph 1, work 2 rows
st st.
Then inc 1 st at beg (back edge) of
next and every row 12 times. *(22 sts)*
Continue straight until left side
of hood measures 14 [16] cm
(5½ [6¼] in), measured at the longer
edge, ending on a p row.
Dec 1 st at beg of next and every
other row 5 times. *(17 sts)*
Cast off.
Right side: Work as for left side but
reverse all shaping.

SLEEVES (MAKE 2)
With 4mm (US 6) needles and wh,
cast on 30 [32] sts.
Work 10 rows k1, p1 rib.
Change to 5mm (US 8) needles.
Beg with a k row and working spot
pattern from graph 1, continue in
st st.
Inc 1 st at each end of next and every
following 4th row 7 times. *(44 [46] sts)*
Continue straight until sleeve
measures 16 [18] cm (6¼ [7] in),
ending on a p row.
SHAPE SLEEVE TOP:
Cast off 3 sts beg of next 2 rows, then
dec 1 st at each end of next and every
other row 4 times. *(30 [32] sts)*
Cast off.

MAKING UP
Block each piece and, using a warm
iron and cloth, press all parts except
ribbing. Sew in ends. Using backstitch
or mattress stitch, sew shoulders
together. Sew right side of hood to
right front of body, and sew left side
of hood to left front of body. Sew
up hood in preparation for adding
the buttonbands.

RIGHT BUTTONBAND
With 4mm (US 6) needles and wh,
pick up 100 [110] sts from crotch of
right front to centre of hood.
Work 5 rows k1, p1 rib.
Cast off.

LEFT BUTTONBAND
Work to match right buttonband
but work row 3 as follows to add
buttonholes:
Row 3: [K1, p1] 1 [2] times, *k2tog, yo,
[k1, p1] 4 times; repeat from * 5 times,
k2tog, yo, rib to end.

EARS (MAKE 2)
With 4mm (US 6) needles and bl,
cast on 3 sts.
Knit 2 rows.
Continue in garter st, inc 1 st at
each end of next and every other
row 3 times. *(9 sts)*
Knit 8 rows.
Cast off.

TO FINISH
Using backstitch or mattress stitch,
set in sleeves and sew up leg, sleeve
and side seams. Sew bottom of
buttonbands to cast-off 4 sts on front.
Join cast-off edges at centre top.
Sew ears to side seams of hood
at curve. Press with a damp cloth.
Sew on buttons.

DACHSHUND BOOTS

MEASUREMENTS
To fit age: 3–6 months
Length: 12cm (4¾in)

MATERIALS
- Pair of 3.25mm (US 3) knitting needles
- 15g (½oz) of Erika Knight British Blue Wool in Pitch – black (bl)
- 5g (⅛oz) of Erika Knight British Blue 100 in Mrs Dalloway – ochre (oc)

TENSION
12 sts and 17 rows to 5cm (2in) measured over st st

BOOTS (MAKE 2)
With bl, cast on 26 sts.
Row 1: Knit.
Row 2: K4, p18, k4.
Rep rows 1–2, 10 times more.
Join in oc.
Row 23: K6bl, k14oc, k6bl.
Row 24: P3bl, p2oc, p1bl, p14oc, p1bl, p2oc, p3bl.
Row 25: K2togbl, k1bl, k2oc, k1bl, k14oc, k1bl, k2oc, k1bl, k2togbl. *(24 sts)*
Row 26: P6bl, p12oc, p6bl.
Row 27: K2togbl, k4bl, k12oc, k4bl, k2togbl. *(22 sts)*
Row 28: P5bl, p12oc, p5bl.
Row 29: K2togbl, k3bl, k12oc, k3bl, k2togbl. *(20 sts)*
Row 30: P5bl, p10oc, p5bl.
Row 31: K2togbl, k3bl, k10oc, k3bl, k2togbl. *(18 sts)*
Row 32: P4bl, p10oc, p4bl.
Row 33: K2togbl, k2bl, k10oc, k2bl, k2togbl. *(16 sts)*
Row 34: P4bl, p8oc, p4bl.
Row 35: K2togbl, k2bl, k8oc, k2bl, k2togbl. *(14 sts)*

Row 36: P3bl, p8oc, p3bl.
Row 37: K2togbl, k1bl, k8oc, k1bl, k2togbl. *(12 sts)*
Row 38: P3bl, p6oc, p3bl.
Cast off in bl.

EARS (MAKE 4)
With bl, cast on 6 sts.
Work 4 rows garter st.
Row 5: Inc, k4, inc. *(8 sts)*
Work 3 rows garter st.
Row 9: Inc, k6, inc. *(10 sts)*
Work 5 rows garter st.
Row 15: K2tog, k6, k2tog. *(8 sts)*
Work 3 rows garter st.
Row 19: K2tog, k4, k2tog. *(6 sts)*
Cast off.

TAIL (MAKE 2)
With bl, cast on 12 sts.
Cast off.

MAKING UP
For each boot, sew up back seam.
Fold boot in half and sew up centre front seam to where garter st edge finishes – approx 7cm (2¾in).
Ears: Sew cast-on edge of ears to boot, one on either side of seam at top edge.
Tail: Sew tail to centre back seam, facing upwards.
Sew in all ends.

PUG BOOTS

MEASUREMENTS
To fit age: 3–6 months
Length: 10cm (4in)

MATERIALS
- Pair of 3.25mm (US 3) knitting needles
- Pair of 2.75mm (US 2) knitting needles
- 15g (½oz) of Erika Knight British Blue Wool in Fawn (fn)
- 10g (¼oz) Erika Knight British Blue Wool in Pitch – black (bl)

TENSION
10 sts and 20 rows to 5cm (2in) measured over garter st using 3.25mm (US 3) needles

BOOTS (MAKE 2)
With 3.25mm (US 3) needles and fn, cast on 26 sts.
Work 30 rows garter st.
Change to bl.
Beg with a k row, continue in st st.
Row 31: K2tog, k22, k2tog. (24 sts)
Row 32: Purl.
Row 33: K2tog, k20, k2tog. (22 sts)
Row 34: Purl.
Row 35: K2tog, k18, k2tog. (20 sts)
Row 36: Purl.
Row 37: K2tog, k16, k2tog. (18 sts)
Row 38: Purl.
Row 39: K2tog, k14, k2tog. (16 sts)
Row 40: Purl.
Row 41: K2tog, k12, k2tog. (14 sts)
Row 42: Purl.
Row 43: K2tog, k10, k2tog. (12 sts)
Work 6 rows st st.
Cast off.

EYES (MAKE 4)
With 2.75mm (US 2) needles and bl, cast on 1 st.
Row 1: [Knit into front and back of st] twice, then knit into front again. (5 sts)
Beg with a p row, work 4 rows st st.
Cast off.

EARS (MAKE 4)
With 2.75mm (US 2) needles and bl, cast on 5 sts.
Beg with a k row, work 5 rows st st.
Cast off.

TAIL (MAKE 2)
For each boot, sew up back seam.
With 3.25mm (US 3) needles and fn and nose of boot facing, pick up and k2 from either side of back seam.
(4 sts)
Beg with a p row, work 14 rows st st.
Cast off.

MAKING UP
Fold each boot in half and sew approx 2.5cm (1in) of fn up from bl across instep. Sew along bl seam and down nose. This sewing-up line sits at the top of the boot.
Nose: Fold back 1cm (⅜in) at end of nose (like a Swiss roll) and catch down where you have folded at second row of fn. With bl, sew 3 satin stitches (straight, parallel stitches worked closely together) across where you have caught down the nose.
Eyes: Sew on eyes, approx 1 row up from fn and 2 sts across from centre seam.
Ears: Sew an ear onto each side of boot, right side up and parallel with centre seam.
Tail: Curl tail outwards and sew down at approx second st from top of centre back seam.
Sew in all ends.

JACK RUSSELL SCARF

MEASUREMENTS
Length: 166cm (65¼in)
Width: 24cm (9½in)

MATERIALS
- Pair of 3.25mm (US 3) knitting needles
- Pair of 4mm (US 6) knitting needles
- 250g (8¾oz) of Erika Knight British Blue Wool in French – mauve (mc)
- 15g (½oz) of Erika Knight British Blue Wool in Milk – cream (cr)
- 10g (¼oz) of Erika Knight British Blue Wool in Milk Chocolate (me)
- Tiny amount of Erika Knight British Blue Wool in Pitch – black (bl) for eye and nose

TENSION
22 sts and 30 rows to 10cm (4in) measured over st st using 4mm (US 6) needles

DOGS ON POCKETS
This scarf is knitted with a Jack Russell (adult size) on each pocket, but you could use any of the dog designs except the Dachshund, which is too long. To choose a different dog, refer to the index of dogs on page 140. This will direct you to the graph for your chosen breed, plus the instructions for knitting the dog onto the front of a jumper, which is where you will find a list of yarn requirements and finishing details for the eyes and nose.

GRAPH
See page 124 for Jack Russell (adult size)

SCARF
With 3.25mm (US 3) needles and mc, cast on 53 sts.
Row 1: [K1, p1] to last st, k1.
This row sets moss st.
Repeat this row 7 times more.
(8 rows in total)
Change to 4mm (US 6) needles.
Next row (RS): [K1, p1] twice, k45, [p1, k1] twice.
Next row (WS): [K1, p1] twice, p45, [p1, k1] twice.
These 2 rows set st st pattern with moss st edge.
Work 4 more rows as set.
Follow graph for Jack Russell, but upside down, starting at the head.

Row 1 of dog: Moss st 4mc, k12mc, k3me, k30mc, moss st 4mc.
Continue as set, following graph pattern until dog is finished.
Work 11 rows as set in mc.
Knit 2 rows to make fold line for first pocket.
Beg with a WS row, work 166cm (65¼in) as set, ending with a RS row.
Knit 2 rows to make fold line for second pocket.
Beg with a p row, work 11 rows as set.
Follow graph for Jack Russell, but this time right way up, starting at the legs.
Row 1 of dog: Moss st 4mc, k9mc, k2me, k17mc, k2me, k15mc, moss st 4mc.

Continue as set, following graph pattern until dog is finished.
Work 6 rows as set in mc.
Change to 3.25mm (US 3) needles.
Work 8 rows moss st.
Cast off.

MAKING UP
At each end of scarf, fold up pocket along garter st fold line and sew up side seams across moss st edge to make a pocket. Lightly press.
Eye: With bl, make a 3-loop French knot for eye.

JACK RUSSELL BOOTS

MEASUREMENTS
To fit age: 3–6 months
Length: 9cm (3½in)

MATERIALS
- Pair of 3.25mm (US 3) knitting needles
- 10g (¼oz) of Erika Knight British Blue Wool in Milk – cream (cr)
- 5g (⅛oz) of Erika Knight British Blue Wool in Milk Chocolate (me)
- Tiny amount of Erika Knight British Blue Wool in Pitch – black (bl) for eyes and nose

TENSION
12 sts and 17 rows to 5cm (2in) measured over st st

BOOTS (MAKE 2)
With cr, cast on 26 sts.
Row 1: Knit.
Row 2: K4, p18, k4.
Rep rows 1–2, 5 times more.
Join in me.
Row 13: K11me, k15cr.
Row 14: K4cr, p10cr, p8me, k4me.
Row 15: K13me, k13cr.
Row 16: K4cr, p9cr, p9me, k4me.
Row 17: K10me, k16cr.
Row 18: K4cr, p7cr, p11me, k4me.
Row 19: K15me, k11cr.
Row 20: K4cr, p7cr, p11me, k4me.
Row 21: K2togme, k13me, k9cr, k2togcr. *(24 sts)*
Row 22: K2togcr, k1cr, p7cr, p11me, k1me, k2togme. *(22 sts)*
Row 23: K2togme, k10me, k8cr, k2togcr. *(20 sts)*
Row 24: K2togcr, p8cr, p8me, k2togme. *(18 sts)*
Row 25: K9me, k9cr.
Row 26: P9cr, p9me.
Cast off in cr.

EARS (MAKE 2 IN CR AND 2 IN ME)
With cr/me, cast on 6 sts.
Work 4 rows garter st.
Row 5: K1, [k2tog] twice, k1. *(4 sts)*
Row 6: [K2tog] twice. *(2 sts)*
Row 7: K2tog and fasten off.

TAIL (MAKE 2)
With cr, cast on 8 sts.
Cast off.

MAKING UP
For each boot, sew up back seam. Fold boot in half and sew up approx 2.5cm (1in) straight up centre front seam, then sew up centre front seam to 2 rows above where me ends.
Ears: Sew cast-on edge of ears to boot, one on either side of centre seam, 2 rows above where centre seam ends. Sew cr ear on cr side, and me ear on me side. Catch down the cast-off edge of each ear.
Eyes: With bl, make a 6-loop French knot for each eye, just below where you have caught down the ears.
Nose: With bl, sew 3 satin stitches (straight, parallel stitches worked closely together) across where the straight part of the centre seam meets top of boot.
Tail: Sew tail to centre back seam, facing upwards.
Sew in all ends.

DOG COAT

MEASUREMENTS

Extra small (XS)
To fit (for example): Chihuahua
Circumference of coat: 32.5cm (12¾in)
Length to polo neck: 30.5cm (12in)

Small (S)
To fit (for example): Jack Russell
Circumference of coat: 39cm (15¼in)
Length to polo neck: 37.5cm (14¾in)

Medium (M)
To fit (for example): Border Collie
Circumference of coat: 46cm (18in)
Length to polo neck: 47.5cm (18¾in)

Large (L)
To fit (for example): Labrador
Circumference of coat: 61cm (24in)
Length to polo neck: 55.5cm (21¾in)

Extra large (XL)
To fit (for example): German Shepherd
Circumference of coat: 70.5cm (27¾in)
Length to polo neck: 61cm (24in)

MATERIALS

- Pair of 4mm (US 6) knitting needles
- Pair of 4.5mm (US 7) knitting needles if using Debbie Bliss yarn or 5mm (US 8) needles if using Cascade yarn
- Debbie Bliss Luxury Tweed Aran or Cascade 220 Aran yarn in main colour (mc) and contrast colour (co)

Size	XS	S	M	L	XL
Main	50g	60g	85g	120g	160g
colour (mc)	(2oz)	(2¼oz)	(3oz)	(4¼oz)	(5½oz)
Contrast	15g	20g	30g	45g	60g
colour (co)	(½oz)	(¾oz)	(1¼oz)	(1¾oz)	(2¼oz)

NOTE: Our dog coat was knitted in size small using Debbie Bliss Luxury Tweed Aran in 53 Meadow (mc) and 15 Charcoal (co)

TENSION
18 sts and 24 rows to 10cm (4in) measured over st st using 4.5mm (US 7) needles for Debbie Bliss yarn or 5mm (US 8) needles for Cascade yarn

TOP OF COAT
With 4mm (US 6) needles and co, cast on 34 [40, 48, 64, 74] sts.
Work 6 rows k1, p1 rib.
Change to larger needles.
Join in mc and continue in st st, working first and last 4 sts in co and st st centre in mc as follows:
Next row (RS): [K1, p1] twice in co, m1 in mc, k26 [32, 40, 56, 66] mc, m1 in mc, [k1, p1] twice in co.
(36 [42, 50, 66, 76] sts)

Next row (WS): [K1, p1] twice in co, p28 [34, 42, 58, 68] mc, [k1, p1] twice in co.
Continue to inc in this way on next and every other row 7 [3, 3, 5, 5] times, and then inc 1 st on every 4th row 0 [5, 5, 6, 8] times.
(50 [58, 66, 88, 102] sts)
This sets pattern of st st centre with 4-st rib border along each side.
Continue straight in st st with rib border until top of coat measures

8 [10, 13, 18, 20] cm (3 [4, 5, 7, 8] in).
Continue in mc and st st only (no rib border) until top of coat measures 14 [19, 28, 33, 36] cm (5½ [7½, 11, 13, 14¼] in), ending on a p row.
MARK LEG OPENINGS:
Mark each end of last row with a coloured thread to indicate beg of leg openings.
Continue in st st until top of coat measures 18.5 [24, 33, 38, 42] cm

(7¼ [9½, 13, 15, 16½] in).
Mark each end of last row with a
coloured thread to indicate end
of leg openings.
Continue in st st until top of coat
measures 25 [31, 40, 45, 50] cm
(10 [12¼, 15¾, 17¾, 19¾] in), ending
on a p row.

SHAPE SHOULDERS:
Next row (RS): K12 [14, 16, 22, 23],
k2tog, k22 [26, 30, 40, 52], k2tog, k12
[14, 16, 22, 23]. *(48 [56, 64, 86, 100] sts)*
Next row (WS): Purl.
Continue to dec in this way, working
2 sts less in centre panel on next and
every other row 4 [5, 5, 11, 13] times.
(40 [46, 54, 64, 74] sts)
Continue in st st until top of coat
measures 30.5 [37.5, 47.5, 55.5, 61] cm
(12 [14¾, 18¾, 21¾, 24] in), ending on
a p row.
Leave rem sts on a holder.

GUSSET
With 4mm (US 6) needles and co,
cast on 14 [18, 24, 30, 34] sts.
Work k1, p1 rib until gusset
measures 6 [9, 15, 15, 16] cm
(2¼ [3½, 6, 6, 6¼] in).

MARK LEG OPENINGS:
Mark each end of last row with a
coloured thread to indicate beg of
leg openings.
Continue in rib, matching
end of leg openings with top
of coat, until gusset measures
19 [24, 28, 30.5, 38] cm
(7½ [9½, 11, 12, 15] in).
Dec 1 st at each end of next and
every other row 3 [4, 6, 8, 9] times.
(8 [10, 12, 14, 16] sts)
Leave rem sts on a holder.

POLO NECK
With 4mm (US 6) needles and
mc and RS facing, rib across

8 [10, 12, 14, 16] sts from holder
for gusset, then rib across
40 [46, 54, 64, 74] sts from holder for
top of coat. *(48 [56, 66, 78, 90] sts)*
Work k1, p1 rib (matching rib
with gusset) until polo neck
measures 11 [12, 13, 13, 14] cm
(4¼ [4¾, 5, 5, 5½] in).
Change to co.
Work 1 row k1, p1 rib.
Cast off loosely in rib.

LEG BANDS
Join gusset from end of leg
openings to neck.
With 4mm (US 6) needles and mc,
pick up 24 [26, 26, 26, 30] sts around

first leg opening, between markers.
Work 6 rows k1, p1 rib.
Change to co.
Work 1 row k1, p1 rib.
Cast off loosely in rib.
Repeat for second leg opening.

MAKING UP
With RS together and matching leg
openings, sew remaining gusset
sides to top of coat. The cast-on
edge of gusset should meet edge of
rib on top of coat. Sew collar seam,
reversing seam on outside for approx
last 6–6.5cm (2¼–2½in) of collar for
turnback. Press gently.

PATCHWORK BABY BLANKET

MEASUREMENTS

Approx 76cm (30in) wide and
100cm (39in) long

MATERIALS

- Pair of 4mm (US 6) knitting needles
- Erika Knight British Blue Wool:
  70g (2½oz) of Milk – cream (cr)
  70g (2½oz) of Sea Fret – light grey (lg)
  60g (2¼oz) of Fawn (fn)
  60g (2¼oz) of Pretty – pale pink (pk)
  50g (2oz) of Iced Gem – aqua (ic)
  50g (2oz) of Mr Bhasin – petrol (mb)
  20g (¾oz) of Pitch – black (bl)
  15g (½oz) of Mouse – grey (mu)
  10g (¼oz) of Milk Chocolate (me)
- Erika Knight British Blue 100:
  50g (2oz) of French – mauve (fr)
  50g (2oz) of Kanoko – pale blue (pb)
- Rowan Kidsilk Haze:
  15g (½oz) of Cream (mohair – mo) – use THREE strands together throughout

TENSION

22 sts and 30 rows to 10cm (4in) measured over st st

NOTE: Our baby blanket is made up of 20 squares, and each square has a moss stitch edge. You can alter the blanket, add initials, leave out the stripes or knit squares with only dogs – in other words, design your own blanket. The squares on the blanket are just the right size for any of the child-size dog breeds except the Dachshund, which is too long. Refer to the blanket plan on page 119 for the exact position of squares and use of colours.

PLAIN SQUARES (MAKE 3)

Cast on 42 sts.
Row 1: [K1, p1] to end.
Row 2: [P1, k1] to end.
Row 3: [K1, p1] to end.
Row 4: P1, k1, p1, k37, p1, k1.
Row 5: K1, p1, k1, p37, k1, p1.
Rows 4–5 set pattern of st st with moss st edges.
Work 52 more rows as set.
(57 rows in total)
Work 3 rows moss st.
Cast off in moss st.

STRIPED SQUARES (MAKE 4)

This square is worked in 4-row stripes of two alternating colours, A and B.
With A, cast on 42 sts.
Row 1: [K1, p1] to end.
Row 2: [P1, k1] to end.
Rows 3–4: Repeat rows 1–2.
Change to B.
Work 4 rows st st with 3 moss sts at each edge (as for plain square).
Continue as set, alternating colours every 4 rows and working 13 stripes in total. *(56 rows in total)*
Change to A.
Work 4 rows moss st as rows 1–4.
Cast off in moss st.

GARTER STITCH RIDGE SQUARES (MAKE 3)

This square is worked in two alternating colours, A and B.
With A, cast on 42 sts and work rows 1–5 as for plain square.
Rows 4–5 set pattern of st st with moss st edges.
Repeat rows 4–5, 3 times more.
Join in B and knit 2 rows in B (these 2 rows make the garter st ridge).
Continue alternating pattern as set and garter st ridges as follows:
• 6 rows A (as set)
• 2 rows B (ridge)
• 4 rows A (as set)
• 2 rows B (ridge)
• 12 rows A (as set)
• 2 rows B (ridge)
• 8 rows A (as set)
• 2 rows B (ridge)
• 4 rows A (as set)
• 2 rows B (ridge)
Change to A and knit 1 row, then work 3 rows moss st as rows 1–3.
Cast off in moss st.

DOG SQUARES (MAKE 10 IN TOTAL)

With main colour (mc), cast on 42 sts and work as for plain square, positioning dog as instructed below.

BORDER COLLIE

Work 3 rows moss st and then 10 rows st st with moss st edges.
Row 14: Moss st 3mc, k8mc, k2bl, k14mc, k3cr, k9mc, moss st 3mc.
Continue graph pattern (page 132) until dog is finished.
Work a further 10 rows in st st with moss st edges.
Work 3 rows moss st and cast off.

DALMATIAN (MAKE 2)

Work 3 rows moss st and then 8 rows st st with moss st edges.
Row 12: Moss st 3mc, k7mc, k2cr, k17mc, k2cr, k8mc, moss st 3mc.
Continue graph pattern (page 133) until dog is finished.
NOTE: The dog's tail will stop at the moss st edge.
Work a further 10 rows in st st with moss st edges.
Work 3 rows moss st and cast off.

JACK RUSSELL

Work 3 rows moss st and then
10 rows st st with moss st edges.
Row 14: Moss st 3mc, k5mc, k2cr,
k17mc, k2cr, k10mc, moss st 3mc.
Continue graph pattern (page 133)
until dog is finished.
Work a further 11 rows in st st with
moss st edges.
Work 3 rows moss st and cast off.

LABRADOR

Work as for Dalmatian using bl
instead of cr (same shape, no spots).
See page 134 for Labrador graph.

PUG (MAKE 2)

Work 3 rows moss st and then
10 rows st st with moss st edges.
Row 14: Moss st 3mc, k6mc, k3bl,
k12mc, k3bl, k12mc, moss st 3mc.
Continue graph pattern (page 134)
until dog is finished.
Work a further 7 rows in st st with
moss st edges.
Work 3 rows moss st and cast off.

WEST HIGHLAND TERRIER

Work 3 rows moss st and then
10 rows st st with moss st edges.
Row 14: Moss st 3mc, k4mc, k4mo,
k14mc, k3mo, k11mc, moss st 3mc.
Continue graph pattern (page 135)
until dog is finished.
Work a further 10 rows in st st with
moss st edges.
Work 3 rows moss st and cast off.

WHIPPET (MAKE 2)

Work 3 rows moss st and then
8 rows st st with moss st edges.
Row 12: Moss st 3mc, k6mc, k2cr,
k17mc, k2cr, k9mc, moss st 3mc.
Continue graph pattern (page 135)
until dog is finished.
Work a further 8 rows in st st with
moss st edges.
Work 3 rows moss st and cast off.

MAKING UP

Using whipstitch, sew the squares
together as positioned on the blanket
plan (see page 119). Try to make
the seams as flat as possible. Add
finishing details if you wish, using
bl or me to sew 3-loop French knots
for eyes, cr to sew slanting stitches
above each of the Pug's eyes and
bl to Swiss darn 1 st for noses.

DALMATIAN
- Main colour (mc) = Sea Fret (light grey – lg)
- Dog = Milk (cream – cr) and Pitch (black – bl)

GARTER STITCH RIDGE SQUARE
- A = Milk (cream – cr)
- B = Iced Gem (aqua – ic)

LABRADOR
- Main colour (mc) = Kanoko (pale blue – pb)
- Dog = Pitch (black – bl)

PLAIN SQUARE
- Mr Bhasin (petrol – mb)

STRIPED SQUARE
- A = Pretty (pale pink – pk)
- B = Milk (cream – cr)

JACK RUSSELL
- Main colour (mc) = French (mauve – fr)
- Dog = Milk (cream cr) and Milk Chocolate (me)

STRIPED SQUARE
- A = Fawn (fn)
- B = Milk (cream – cr)

WEST HIGHLAND TERRIER
- Main colour (mc) = Pretty (pale pink – pk)
- Dog = Cream mohair (mo)

PUG
- Main colour (mc) = Milk (cream – cr)
- Dog = Fawn (fn) and Pitch (black – bl)

PLAIN SQUARE
- Pretty (pale pink – pk)

WHIPPET
- Main colour (mc) = Kanoko (pale blue – pb)
- Dog = Milk (cream – cr) and Mouse (grey – mu)

GARTER STITCH RIDGE SQUARE
- A = Iced Gem (aqua – ic)
- B = Mr Bhasin (petrol – mb)

PLAIN SQUARE
- Sea Fret (light grey – lg)

BORDER COLLIE
- Main colour (mc) = Iced Gem (aqua – ic)
- Dog = Pitch (black – bl) and Milk (cream – cr)

GARTER STITCH RIDGE SQUARE
- A = Sea Fret (light grey – lg)
- B = Milk Chocolate (me)

DALMATIAN
- Main colour (mc) = French (mauve – fr)
- Dog = Milk (cream – cr) and Pitch (black – bl)

WHIPPET
- Main colour (mc) = Fawn (fn)
- Dog = Milk (cream – cr) and Mouse (grey – mu)

STRIPED SQUARE
- A = Mouse (grey – mu)
- B = Pretty (pale pink – pk)

PUG
- Main colour (mc) = Mr Bhasin (petrol – mb)
- Dog = Fawn (fn) and Pitch (black – bl)

STRIPED SQUARE
- A = Fawn (fn)
- B = Kanoko (pale blue – pb)

ADULT SIZE

BEAGLE

▨	black (bl)
▨	gold (gd)
☐	white (wh)
⦁⦁⦁	black (bl)
▧	background

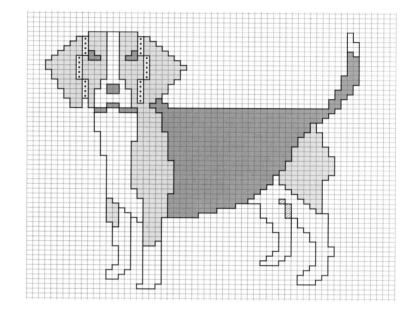

BORDER COLLIE

▨	black (bl)
☐	white (wh)
⦁⦁⦁	background

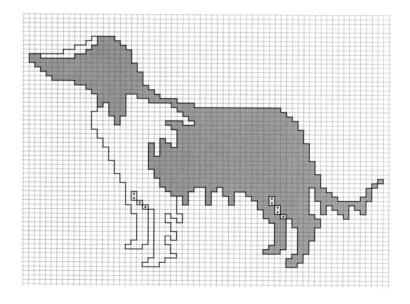

BORDER TERRIER

- coffee (co)
- background
- charcoal (ch)

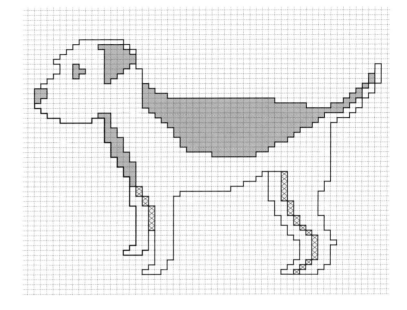

CHIHUAHUA

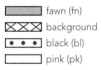

- fawn (fn)
- background
- black (bl)
- pink (pk)

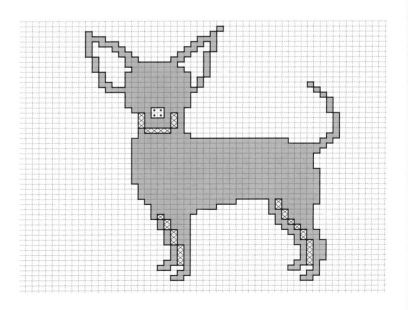

ADULT SIZE

DACHSHUND

- ⨯⨯⨯ gold (gd)
- ▨ black (bl)
- ⊡•⊡ background

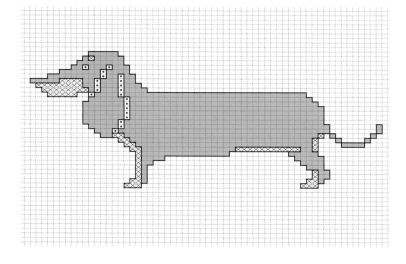

DALMATIAN

- ▭ white (wh)
- ▨ black (bl)

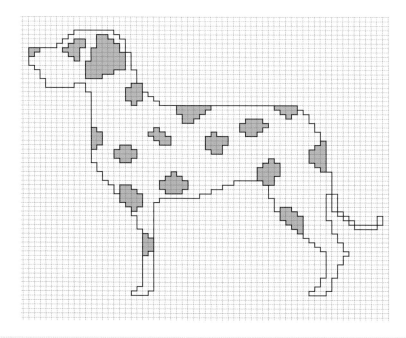

FRENCH BULLDOG

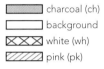

- charcoal (ch)
- background
- white (wh)
- pink (pk)

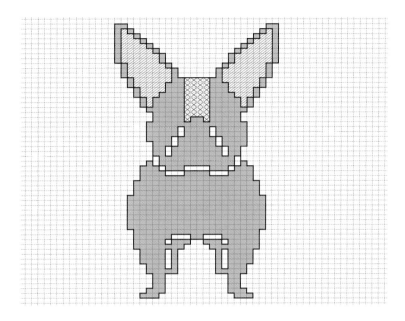

GOLDEN RETRIEVER

- fawn (fn)
- black (bl)
- background

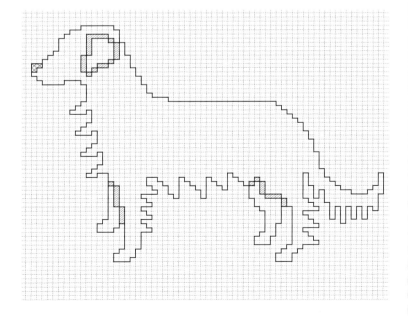

ADULT SIZE

JACK RUSSELL

cream (cr)

fawn (fn)

black (bl)

background

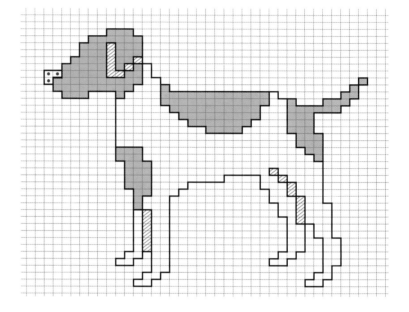

LABRADOODLE

white bouclé (ow)

background

black (bl)

NOTE: Swiss darn the eyes

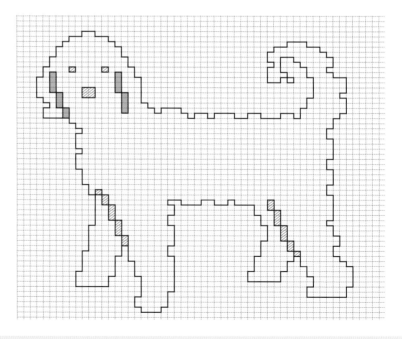

LABRADOR

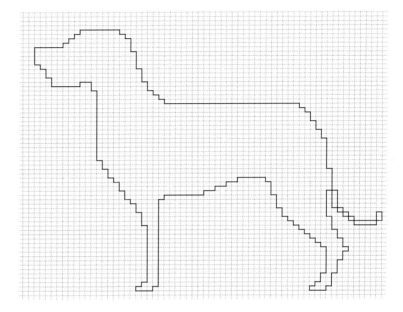

| | black (bl) |

LURCHER

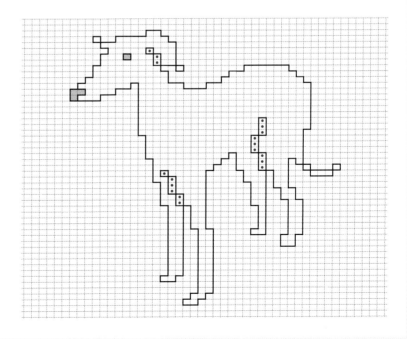

	4 strands mohair (mo)
• • •	background
	charcoal (ch)

ADULT SIZE

MINIATURE SCHNAUZER

- ▭ 4 strands mohair (mo)
- ▨ background
- ▨ grey (gr)
- ▨ black (bl)
- • • • loopy stitch using 4 strands mohair (mo)

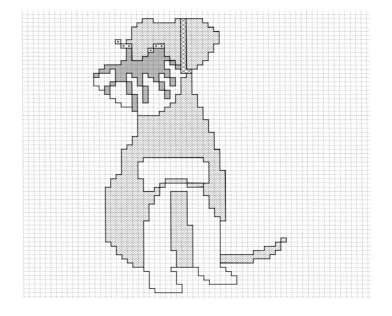

PUG

- ▭ oval colour
- ▭ oatmeal (oa)
- • • • oval or background colour
- ▨ charcoal (ch)

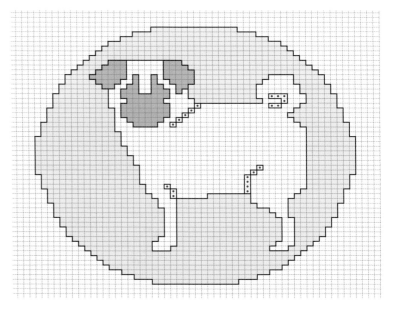

SPRINGER SPANIEL

mahogany (ma)
white (wh)
black (bl)
background

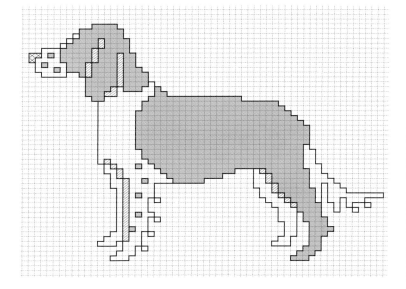

STAFFORDSHIRE BULL TERRIER

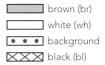

brown (br)
white (wh)
background
black (bl)

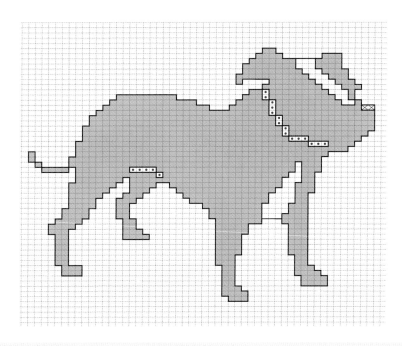

ADULT SIZE

WEST HIGHLAND TERRIER

	4 strands mohair (mo)
	black (bl)
✕✕✕	pink (pk)

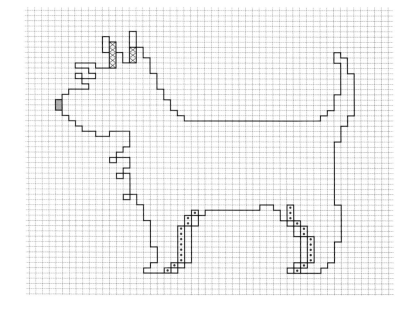

WHIPPET

	white (wh)
///	background
	fawn (fn)
✕✕✕	black (bl)

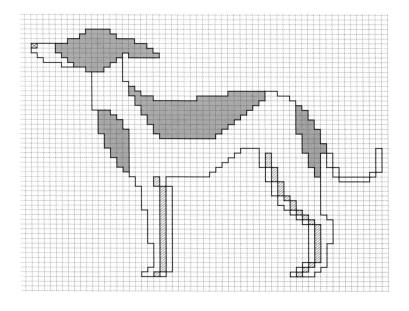

CAVE CANEM

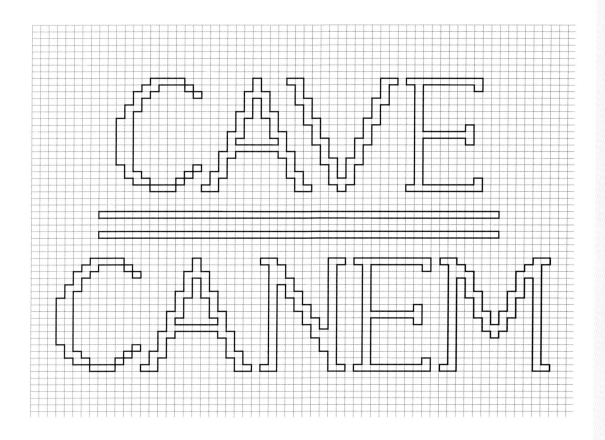

□ white (wh)

ALPHABET

CHILD/BABY SIZE

BORDER COLLIE

☐ cream (cr)
▨ black (bl)

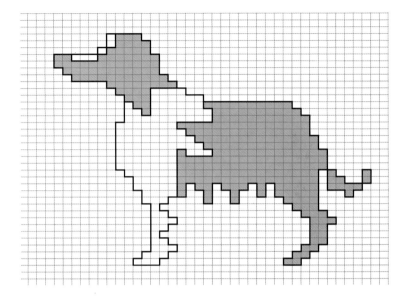

DACHSHUND

☐ black (bl)
⊠ ochre (oc)
⊡ cream (cr)

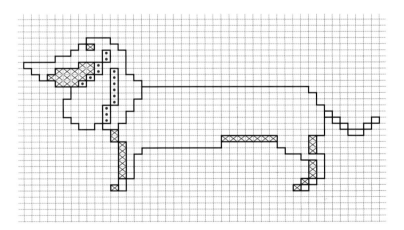

DALMATIAN

cream (cr)
black (bl)

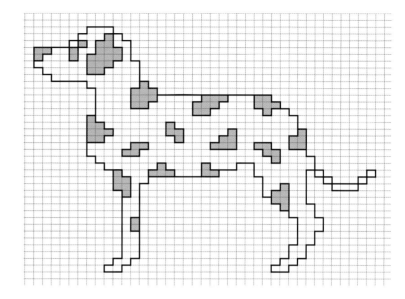

JACK RUSSELL

oval colour
cream (cr)
• • • cream (cr)
milk chocolate (me)
oval or background colour

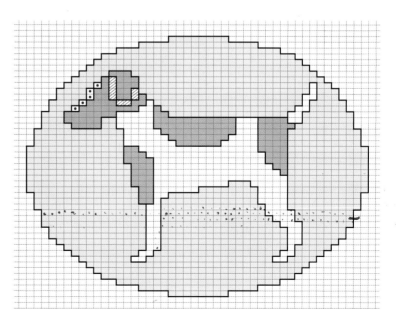

CHILD/BABY SIZE

LABRADOR

black (bl)

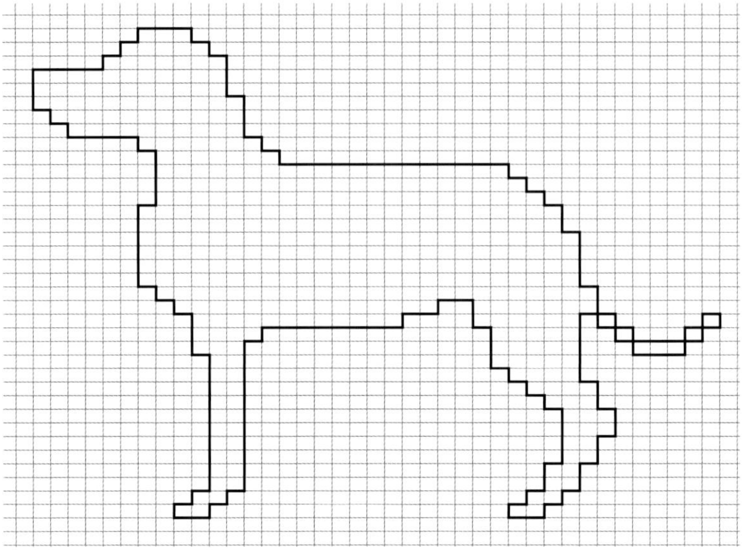

PUG

fawn (fn)
background
black (bl)

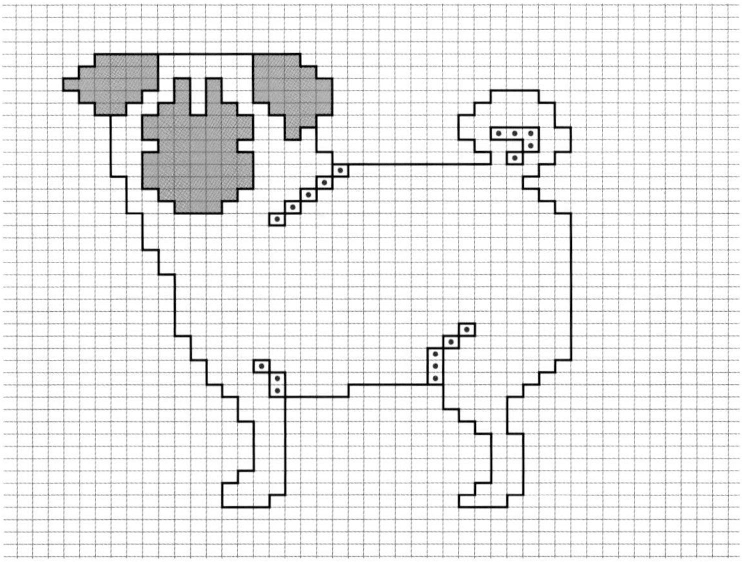

WEST HIGHLAND
TERRIER

▭	3 strands mohair (mo)
⌧	black (bl)

NOTE: Swiss darn the nose

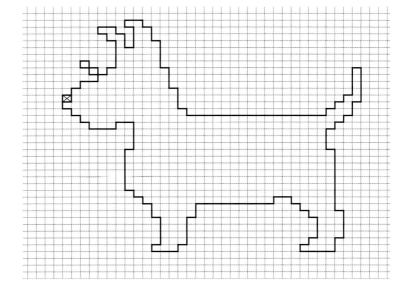

WHIPPET

▭	cream (cr)
▨	grey (mu)
⌧	black (bl)

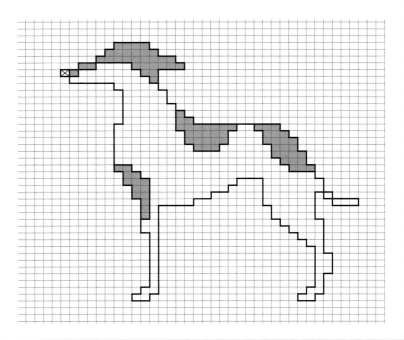

BABY'S CARDIGAN

JACK RUSSELL

 cream (cr)

 milk chocolate (me)

cream (cr)

background

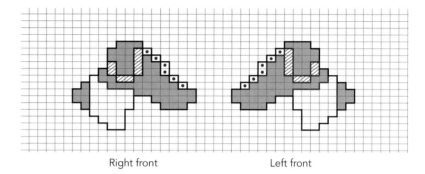

Right front   Left front

MINIATURE SCHNAUZER

3 strands mohair (mo)

background

grey (mu)

black (bl)

loopy stitch using 3 strands
mohair (mo)

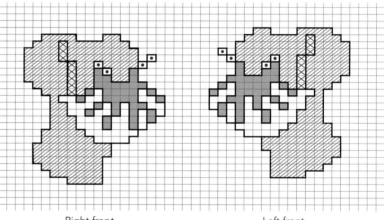

Right front   Left front

DACHSHUND

black (bl)

ochre (oc)

background

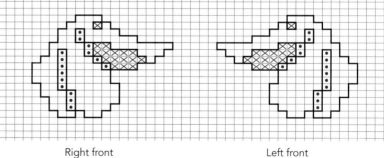

Right front   Left front

DALMATIAN ONESIE

GRAPH 1

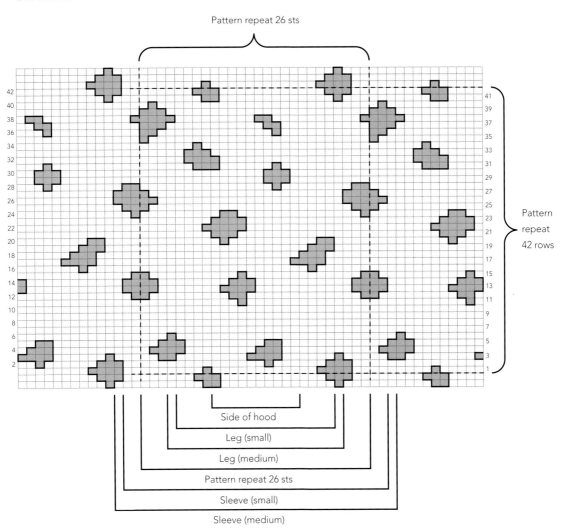

Pattern repeat 26 sts

42 40 38 36 34 32 30 28 26 24 22 20 18 16 14 12 10 8 6 4 2

41 39 37 35 33 31 29 27 25 23 21 19 17 15 13 11 9 7 5 3 1

Pattern repeat 42 rows

Side of hood

Leg (small)

Leg (medium)

Pattern repeat 26 sts

Sleeve (small)

Sleeve (medium)

DALMATIAN ONESIE

GRAPH 2

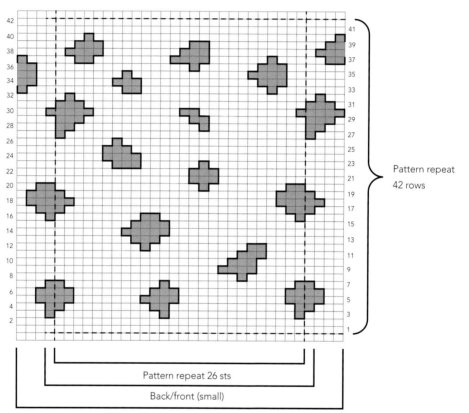

Pattern repeat
42 rows

Pattern repeat 26 sts

Back/front (small)

Back/front (medium)

INDEX OF DOGS

Adult sizes	Width	Height	Yarn and instructions	Graph
Beagle	51 sts	54 rows	page 32	page 120
Border Collie	62 sts	52 rows	page 58	page 120
Border Terrier	55 sts	48 rows	page 56	page 121
Cave Canem	58 sts	44 rows	page 64	page 129
Chihuahua	39 sts	50 rows	page 42	page 121
Dachshund	60 sts	30 rows	page 62	page 122
Dalmatian	62 sts	60 rows	page 34	page 122
French Bulldog	26 sts	56 rows	page 38	page 123
Golden Retriever	65 sts	56 rows	page 40	page 123
Jack Russell	36 sts	37 rows	page 50	page 124
Labradoodle	48 sts	55 rows	page 48	page 124
Labrador	62 sts	60 rows	page 28	page 125
Lurcher	36 sts	47 rows	page 30	page 125
Miniature Schnauzer	35 sts	65 rows	page 52	page 126
Pug	35 sts	40 rows	page 36	page 126
Springer Spaniel	57 sts	49 rows	page 44	page 127
Staffordshire Bull Terrier	52 sts	49 rows	page 46	page 127
West Highland Terrier	44 sts	46 rows	page 60	page 128
Whippet	57 sts	52 rows	page 54	page 128
Child/baby sizes				
Border Collie	36 sts	34 rows	page 90	page 132
Dachshund	46 sts	25 rows	page 86	page 132
Dalmatian	39 sts	36 rows	page 82	page 133
Jack Russell	34 sts	33 rows	page 92	page 133
Labrador	39 sts	36 rows	page 84	page 134
Pug	32 sts	37 rows	page 88	page 134
West Highland Terrier	34 sts	34 rows	page 80	page 135
Whippet	34 sts	38 rows	page 94	page 135
Additional graph designs				
Alphabet	–	17 rows	page 64	page 130
Baby's cardigan	–	–	page 72	page 136
Dalmatian onesie	–	–	page 102	pages 137, 138

ABBREVIATIONS

approx	approximately		**oz**	ounce(s)
beg	begin(ning)		**p**	purl
cm	centimetre(s)		**p2tog**	purl next two stitches together
dec	knit (purl) two stitches together to decrease by one stitch		**rem**	remain(ing)
			rep	repeat
g	gram(s)		**RS**	right side
in	inch(es)		**st(s)**	stitch(es)
inc	work in the front and back of next stitch to increase by one stitch		**st st**	stocking stitch
			WS	wrong side
k	knit		**yo**	yarn over
k2tog	knit next two stitches together		**[ ]**	square brackets either contain instructions or information relating to larger sizes in multiple-size patterns, or indicate instructions to be worked as directed after the closing bracket
m1	from the front, use tip of left needle to pick up horizontal strand of yarn between last stitch worked and next stitch, then knit through back of it to make one stitch			
mm	millimetre(s)		*****	work instructions after asterisk(s) as directed

RESOURCES

Cascade Yarn is an American company, available in the UK online from:
- www.woolwarehouse.co.uk
- www.loveknitting.com

Erika Knight, Debbie Bliss and Rowan yarns are available from most good wool shops and online from:
- www.deramores.co.uk
- www.loveknitting.co.uk

Drops Alpaca Bouclé yarn is available from:
- www.woolwarehouse.co.uk

These are the yarns we recommend, but any aran or double-knit weight would be a good substitute, so do ask your wool shop for a recommendation. Yarn companies are forever evolving and changing their ranges, so although some colours may be discontinued, there is always an alternative.

PHOTOGRAPHY CREDITS

Ursula Aitchison of Phodography:
Cover photography and images on pages 4, 7, 11, 12, 13, 14, 17, 19, 21, 29, 31, 33, 35, 37, 39, 41, 43, 45, 47, 49, 51, 53, 55, 57, 59, 61, 63, 65, 66, 69, 71, 73 (top right), 73 (bottom right), 81, 83, 85, 87, 89, 91, 93, 95, 96, 100, 103, 107, 109, 113, 115, 131, 139, 142 and 144.

Martin Norris: images on pages 22, 23, 24, 25, 26, 27, 73 (left), 76, 77, 78, 79, 98, 99, 110, 111 and 118.

ACKNOWLEDGEMENTS

Many people have been involved in the making of this book and we would like to profusely thank Krissy Mallett for her endless encouragement, calming nature and spreadsheet skills; Katie Cowan for loyally commissioning this book; Michelle Pickering for editing the book into shape; Marilyn Wilson for her brilliant forensic pattern checking; Michelle Mac and Sophie Yamamoto for working magic with the design; Kuo Kang Chen for drawing our graphs so brilliantly; Martin Norris for his attention to detail; Lindsey Poole for the beautiful make-up and hair; and the wonderful Ursula Aitchison of Phodography for her glorious lifestyle photography and excellent dog whispering skills (www.phodography.org.uk).

A huge thank you to Cascade in the US and Erika Knight in the UK for their amazing yarns and generosity in supporting this book.

Thank you too to our understanding and expert knitters, Deidre, Sheila, Lyn, Rosemary, Sylvia and her team.

We have asked and cajoled quite a few friends and friends of friends to model the knitwear and bring along their wonderful dogs, so a huge thank you must go to: Abigail, Albert, Audrey, Audrey B, Bella, Beth, Betsy, Caitlin, Caroline, Cilla, Clover, Daisy, Daniel B, Daniel T, Dougal, Dylan, Eliza, Elsie, Ember, Etienne, Felix, Figgie, Florence C, Florence K, Francesca, Fred, Frida, Gracie, Gregory, Henry, Herbie, Huxley, Jeremy, Jessica B, Jessica E, Jo, Junior, Katherine, Katy, Kelly, Kim, Laurie, Louise G, Louise P, Lucky, Maude, Maxx, Michael, Mick, Mike, Millie, Molly, Morgan, Oscar, Oscar M-H, Patrick, Pegasus, Percy, Peter, Phoenix, Poppy, Ramona, Rooney, Siobhan, Spice, Stanley, Steph, Susan, Suzanna, Ted, Theo, Wilfred, Winnie, Zoe, Zoe L and, of course, the remarkable Hugo.

Sally Muir and Joanna Osborne are co-authors of the bestselling *Best in Show* series of knitting books. This is their tenth book and combines their two great interests: knitting and dogs. They have run their own knitwear business, Muir and Osborne, for many years, exporting to stores in the United States, Japan and Europe as well as selling to shops in the United Kingdom. Several pieces of their knitwear are in the permanent collection at the Victoria and Albert Museum, London, including their red sheep jumper as worn by Princess Diana.

To see the books and current collection, go to www.muirandosborne.co.uk or follow us on Instagram @muirandosborne